One of the nation's most distinguished scholars offers here, distilled from a lifetime of observation, a great statement of the moderate view of society.

The role of government in the economic sphere is the overriding question of our time. The course of civilization turns on the answer.

Professor MacIver believes that modern states have been developing a middle way between socialism and capitalism as the inevitable result of new situations and new conditions. Should we go all the way to socialism, democracy would be in mortal danger. But those who ignore the demands of the people for social security and freedom from economic discrimination are also the enemies of democracy.

This thoughtful book comprises a series of lectures delivered on the William W. Cook Foundation at the University of Michigan.

THE
WILLIAM W. COOK FOUNDATION
LECTURES

Earlier volumes in this series were:

FREEDOM AND RESPONSIBILITY IN
THE AMERICAN WAY OF LIFE
by Carl L. Becker
[1945]

TOTAL WAR AND THE CONSTITUTION
by Edward S. Corwin
[1947]

ALTERNATIVE TO SERFDOM
by John Maurice Clark
[1948]

MEN AND MEASURES IN THE LAW
by Arthur T. Vanderbilt
[1949]

CHARACTERISTICALLY AMERICAN
by Ralph Barton Perry
[1949]

THESE ARE *Borzoi Books*
PUBLISHED BY *Alfred A. Knopf* IN NEW YORK

Democracy and the Economic Challenge

THE WILLIAM W. COOK FOUNDATION was established at the University of Michigan to endow a distinguished Lectureship on American Institutions. The donor, William Wilson Cook, long a member of the New York bar, received the degree of Bachelor of Arts from the College of Literature, Science, and the Arts of the University in 1880, and the degree of Bachelor of Laws from the Law School in 1882.

The lectures presented in this volume are the sixth in the series of lectures under the Foundation. They were delivered in the Rackham lecture halls at the University in December 1950, and are published, under a special arrangement between the University and the publisher, as the sixth volume in the lectureship series.

The first volume was Freedom and Responsibility in the American Way of Life, *by Carl L. Becker; the second volume was* Total War and the Constitution, *by Edward S. Corwin; the third was* Alternative to Serfdom, *by John Maurice Clark; the fourth was* Men and Measures in the Law, *by Arthur T. Vanderbilt; the fifth was* Characteristically American, *by Ralph Barton Perry.*

Democracy

AND THE

Economic Challenge

Five lectures delivered on the William W. Cook Foundation
at the University of Michigan, December 1950

By ROBERT M. MacIVER

New York   *ALFRED A. KNOPF*   1952

L. C. CATALOG CARD NUMBER: 51-13213

THIS IS A BORZOI BOOK,
PUBLISHED BY ALFRED A. KNOPF, INC.

FIRST EDITION

Foreword

IN PRESENTING this addition to the volumes of the University of Michigan Law School's William W. Cook Foundation Lectures I take the opportunity to express to Dean E. Blythe Stason, his colleagues of the Law School, and the other members of the University of Michigan, staff and student, my grateful remembrance of the hospitality and friendly interest that made the giving of these addresses a happy occasion for the author.

R. M. MacIver

Contents

I. Public and Private Economic Power   3

II. The Rise of Private Economic Power   20

III. The Portent of Karl Marx   35

IV. Democracy and the Planned Economy   51

V. The Meaning for America   71

INDEX   *follows page*   86

Democracy and the Economic Challenge

I

Public and Private
Economic Power

1

THE CENTRAL CONFLICT of the twentieth century rages and in the calculable future, if such there be, will continue to rage over a question of political economy, over the question of the proper role of government in the economic area. The issue is tangled by the extraordinary historical changes brought about by the most destructive wars in the record of mankind. All kinds of allegiances and rivalries and interests and sentiments are bound up with it, and looming over them all is the eternal drive of the powerful for power. But the conflict itself focuses in an economic challenge that first was given expression in the nineteenth century and has reached its apex in our own days. At first the issue was raised within various countries. But now it has taken for its stage the international scene.

There were of course politico-economic conflicts in earlier times. There has been from of old the struggle of the poor against the exactions of the rich, of the land-hungry against feudal landlords. There have been occasional slave risings and peasant revolts. There have been the more continuous conflicts of economic group against economic group, conflicts for economic advantage and conflicts against economic privilege, renewed in changing forms up to the present day. But all these issues have been different

3

from this final issue. They did not reach down to the very foundation of authority, the basis of social order. The problem of the relation of society to property has gone through many stages. The present stage is climactic; it has a more profound significance than was possessed by any earlier stage.

To bring out its meaning is the purpose of these chapters. There is much misunderstanding concerning it. The memories and traditions of older conflicts confuse our perception of it. To help to make the difference clear I shall first present a series of thumbnail sketches depicting various stages in the relation of society and property.

1. We begin with very simple societies, the small nearly insulated close-to-nature societies where the means of production are the simple tools of a handicraft age—except, of course, the land on which they live, where each family provides most of its own supplies, where economic exchange is often the mere barter of surplus goods, and where most of the products of labor are for the direct satisfaction of physiological needs.

These simple peoples, outside of the contact of modern civilization, are by our standards poor peoples, whether they live in the lush tropics or in the arctic snows or anywhere in between. The earth is niggard to simple peoples, niggard and unpredictable.

When a people is poor they do not struggle among themselves for wealth. They do not contemplate the possibility of changing their lot in life. The opportunity hardly presents itself. They do not think about rising in the world. The day's work ends with the day, and tomorrow it is more of the same. They do not think in economic terms. They have no working hours set apart. Labor is often hard and the fruits are nearly always scanty. The life of the family and the field or the forest encompasses them. They live as families and share the patrimonial earth. Its ownership

4

is at once familial and communal. It is hard to say what is ownership and what is only usufruct.

These simple peoples do not hire servants, do not have employees. They do not seek slaves through conquest. What would they do with them? They want no more mouths to feed. The tribal chief may have a henchman or two, but there is little difference, except the ceremonial one, between his way of living and that of the tribesmen. He is the leader, he is the judge. He gets the choicest portion when there is something to divide.

At this stage economic power, whether private or public, is negligible. The chief, the medicine man, the elders exercise some power, because of their authority as interpreters of the customary law, as judges, as giving guidance and leadership to the folk. But their power has no basis in economic conditions.

2. Let us look at a second stage. It is an agricultural society. It has acquired a greater variety of arts. It has learned to prepare the soil, to select seed, and to breed cattle. There are leading men who have larger herds and broader lands, like the patriarchs of the Old Testament. Social organization is more developed. There is rank, there are social classes. The tribe, in its occasional wars, often mere raiding expeditions, has brought back captives, to become slaves of the chief and his subordinates.

Authority is now accompanied by superior wealth. There is a rather direct relation between status and property. The leaders are able to increase their possessions. Their families become an elite. They have household servants and slaves and hired workers. A demarcation arises between the landed classes and the landless. The landless become the tillers of the soil, the hewers of wood and drawers of water for the superior class. Economic power combines with tribal authority, supports it, and expands its range.

But authority is rarely questioned, for it is inherent in

the ways of the tribe. Authority was not derived in the first place from economic power, though it is now buttressed and greatly expanded through the acquisition of this increasingly differentiated power. But the habit of acceptance is already rooted in the mores. The kinship system, as well as the enlarged patriarchal household, protects the individual against hunger, so long as there is anything to share. There are no detached individuals in this kind of society, no familyless men, no unemployed. There are economic quarrels between the leaders, sometimes resulting in violence. There are grievances of the poor against the rich. There is the sullen muttering of the slave. But there is no suggestion that the system is wrong. The establishment is secure.

3. Let us move forward a step, up the ladder of social organization. Here and there the successful agricultural society becomes a village. Several such villages arise within an area, within the range of communication and trade. One has a more favorable location. It is situated, say, at a bend of a river in a fertile valley or at a location fortified by nature or with near access to a convenient port or at the intersection of trading routes. Thus it grows stronger and wealthier, gathers the neighborhood to itself, and becomes a city. It becomes at the same time a center of government, with dominion over a hinterland. Where there are wide plains around it, it becomes the mother city of a small empire. Where mountains or sea inlets break the land, it becomes a city-state.

Thus came into being many of the famous cities that have been the nurses of all our civilization. Thus arose Ur and Nippur of the Sumerians, thus arose Babylon and Kish and Nineveh and Tyre, Knossos and Mycenæ and Tiryns and Troy, Athens and Corinth and Argos and Sparta, the Egyptian Thebes, Rome and Carthage, and in the Western World Tenochtitlán and the Inca Cuzco.

The city is no longer agricultural, as was the village. It is the home of the rulers. It is a market place. It is the focus of the arts and crafts. In it new ways of living arise, far removed from the ways of "nature." The city is changeful and restless. In it wealth is more quickly acquired and sometimes more quickly lost. In it the struggle for power takes on new dimensions.

Outside it, in the hinterland, the cultivators follow their old ways. But now they pay tribute to the city, to which they send a portion of all they produce. The cultivators are peasants, and the peasant lives an utterly different life from the townsman. In the changeful cities history is made. The peasant is outside of history, except that he is also its victim.

Among their other arts the cities had the art of domination. They contained, before quite modern times, only a small percentage of the population. The vast majority were country-dwellers. Even today, over great portions of the earth, in eastern Europe, in Russia, in China and India, in Latin America, in the more arable portions of Africa, most men are cultivators of the soil. They have gone, with scarcely perceptible changes, their immemorial way. They still do so except where the intrusive forces of the urban civilization, with their ever more powerful means of communication and indoctrination, lay hold on them.

4. What I have given is a mere schematic outline of a complicated process. Out of the conditions mentioned, as a result of wars and a thousand vicissitudes, responsive also to new development of the arts and crafts, the greater oligarchies arose, the empires and dynasties the record of which fills the pages of the history books.

Sometimes these great oligarchies had their focus in a single city, once a city-state, like Babylon and Thebes and Rome. Sometimes they were more loosely organized in tiered hierarchies, the feudal type that spread in the Orient

7

and over medieval Europe. But always there was characteristically the sharp distinction between the ruling class, the elite of power and property that owned the land, and the large subject class of the cultivators, the peasants.

Under these conditions property and authority were conjoined. You could not distinguish economic power from political power. Any proposal that government should take over economic control would have been meaningless. The government was in the hands of the class that owned all wealth. The possession of economic power was one aspect of the total establishment. The establishment, the class-bound social order, held in extricable union position and possession and power. *Economic power was also public power,* except for minor and temporary deviations. There was practically no place for private economic power—that is, economic control in the hands of individuals or groups who did not at the same time and over the same range possess political authority as well. If you were a landowner you possessed thereby a corresponding degree of political authority. If you ran any important enterprise it was most likely on governmental concession. And practically the only way to acquire much wealth, in these pre-capitalistic times, was to be appointed to some political position. At Rome, for example, the best road to affluence was through appointment as a proconsul of one of the provinces.

The line was drawn between the private poverty of the unprivileged, the subject class, and the politically derived wealth of the ruling class. There was often strife between these classes, stirred by the restless discontent of the poor, especially in those societies where civilization was most advanced. In ancient Greece, for example, every city, said the historian Thucydides, became two cities, one of the rich and the other of the poor. It was so also in Rome, where the plebeians, the politically unprivileged, twice attempted to migrate in mass and to found a new city. But the cry was against oppression and ruinous taxation and intolerable burdens of debts—not against the social order itself. In the advanced city-states the poor citizens sought to enter the circle of the privileged, to share the politico-economic power. In Athens and then in Rome they succeeded for a time in getting a share of it. That is what ancient democracy meant—except for the new principle it proclaimed. In effect it meant that the poorer citizens were admitted to the ruling class, as against the peasants, the resident aliens, and the slaves. Ancient democracy was still only an enlarged oligarchy.

Nowhere in that older world do we find any important role played by private economic power, economic power dissociated from government itself. An interesting transitional stage is displayed by various Latin-American republics that proclaim a fully democratic constitution but because of the poverty and illiteracy of the population and other adverse conditions are actually governed by unstable army-supported cliques. Under these conditions the *politicos* are profit-making partners, as it were, in all important business and financial enterprises. The government does not itself run the business of the country, but it is in on every deal and nothing can be accomplished without its express support, which means without its having a voice in the matter and a prior share in the benefits thereof. The politicos and the men of affairs are always hand in hand, a system that takes a heavy tribute from the public at large.

To resume, in all the political systems of the past, until modern democracy grew into being, political authority and property-ownership, economic power and political power, were blended or fused. It is a favorite theory of the Marxists, though it is not confined to them, that government rested wholly on economic power and was merely an instrument of control in the service of the property-owners. This kind of simplification is easy and no doubt beguiling. Two

9

things become inextricably combined—it is an old dialectical trick to affirm that one is wholly the cause or the instrument or the condition of the other. Authority is more deep-seated in human nature and in human needs than this facile dogma realizes. For our purpose here it is enough to say that economic power, particularly the power of landownership, became in the rise and maintenance of these oligarchies an important bulwark anchored in the very foundations of authority. Political power and economic power were indistinguishable. Neither existed apart from the other. There were occasional times of crisis in which a political convulsion occurred that for a brief historical moment threatened to separate them. An upstart ruler, risen from the lower ranks, might thus win political power, but that very fact soon endowed him and his entourage with economic power, the power of ownership as well.

It was of course natural that the ruling class should veil the role of economic power in the maintenance of their authority. Instead they invoked their God-given right and their own intrinsic superiority, of descent, of distinction, of achievement, of service. There was indeed one aspect of their position that they could least afford to admit, the aspect that the revolutionary spirit, as it gained confidence, claimed to be the whole explanation. They could not admit that their display, their great mansions, their bodyguards, their armies, were made possible only by the labor of the subject classes, that in this sense they lived off these classes. This part of the truth, which in turn was presented as the whole truth by the revolutionary movements of the nineteenth century, they conveniently ignored. Instead they perpetuated the appropriate myths, the myths of sovereignty and of rank and of investiture and of the divinity that doth hedge a king, the myth of the eternal order in which all men have their appointed place, the myth of the primary obligation of obedience to the powers that be. In the traditional thought-forms economic power was merely the corollary, the appendage, of political authority.

It could not have been otherwise. In the earlier world, given the conditions and given human nature, it was inevitable that power should depend on weakness and that wealth should fatten on poverty. Thus only, under the conditions, could ambition advance, thus only could order be established. A better order, a greater society, had to wait until man's ingenuity had opened the road toward abundance. With handicraft technology there was not enough wealth to raise the general standard much above subsistence level.

This, then, was the state of affairs throughout far the greater part of recorded history. Authority and property and position were united in a single focus of power. Each of the trinity sustained the other two. Each blended into the other two. Take property, for example. It has a three-way impact on society. In the first place, it commands goods and services; that is, it makes other men dependent on its possessor in the very act of serving him—this is economic power in its direct application. In the second place, in those earlier times at least, it commands a body of followers or retainers who in effect are the subjects of its possessor— this is the political application. In the third, it commands the means of display and distinction and luxury, the symbols of rank. This is the social application. Thus economic power reinforced political power and confirmed social status. This triple command separated the ruling classes from the masses.

2

Such was the old order of things. Out of it, as changing conditions stirred new movements among the people, there gradually emerged a new order, the order of the democratic state. Of primary importance in bringing it into fuller being was technological change, the practical control over the forces of nature that harnessed them to the service of human wants. This change gave new potency to ideas of justice and freedom and political equality and equal opportunity that had often been frustrated before. So long as poverty was the lot of the vast majority, as it was until recent times, as it still is today over large parts of the earth, the old order stood firm or, if it was upset by some conjuncture of forces, it was restored under another name.

Here and there a trading people, occupying a strategic position, acquired resources that fell in part into the hands of those who did not belong to the ruling classes—for trade was generally regarded as petty business and therefore below the level of their dignity. These resources therefore remained private economic power. Where that happened the old order received its first onslaught, as in England, for reasons I shall later develop. But it was not until the rise of modern industry that the ancient union of property and authority was fully and finally challenged. It was only then that modern democracy came into its own.

Industrial development brought a complex of deep-working changes that, as their impact took effect, fatally undermined the ancient formula, the hallowed trinity of authority and property and social class. In the first place the new wealth, the swiftly moving and cumulating wealth of industry, capital, was acquired by the middle and not the upper classes. Manufacture and its trading component were not congenial to the aristocracy; it was a lower-class occupation, unfit for gentlemen. Only property in land had social prestige. So the middle classes expanded in numbers and in power. And since capital wealth is susceptible of indefinite increase, since, in the words of Karl Marx, "capital is a monster that is fruitful and multiplies," the aristocratic landowner began to lose out to the manufacturer and

12

the merchant, and presently to save his heritage he began to enter into matrimonial alliances with the new-rich and to adorn with his name the lists of company directors. The balance of power was changing and the old class structure was shaken out of its rigidity.

In the second place, the advance of technology that attended and stimulated the new industrial development brought men into new relationships and created new kinds of organization and therewith new kinds of power. It fostered new habits of work, new ways of thought, new attitudes. It meant liberation from old usages and traditions and at the same time it imposed new compulsions that flouted old ordinances. Technology is the most subtle and the most effective engineer of enduring social change. Its apparent neutrality is deceptive and often disarming. The cultural implications of the new industry were adverse to the hitherto scarcely challenged culture of which the upper classes were the guardians and beneficiaries. It was fatal to the doctrines that bulwarked the class-bound society.

Ancient prestige felt the shock of industrial power. One area in which the impact struck deep was that of the military structure. The army was the "last argument of kings," not only in international but also in domestic affairs. The oligarchy of the throne was of necessity guarded by the army. The upper class was also the officer class. But birth and ancestral acres gave no fitness to command in the days of mechanized warfare. Napoleon in the earliest days of mechanization already made the message very clear. Moreover, as mechanization advanced, a warrior class became an anachronism. Qualities of leadership and professional talent became too important, wherever they appeared, to be ignored for lack of "blue blood." Moreover, the demands of war became so many-sided that the whole people were drawn in. Warfare ceased to be an occupation pursued for glory and honor. Mechanism and high explosives took the fabled glamour out of it. Necessity overpowered tradition.

The military caste resisted the trend but could not stay it. Remnants of the tradition remain here and there. Each new war has reduced them further. In Germany the resistance was particularly strong, but in the end a mere corporal, a man of the people, ignorant and headstrong and a devotee of the rabid nationalism that worshipped another idol than that of caste, became the blind instrument of the destruction of the system.

The new conditions, the new habituations, the new necessities everywhere bred doctrines hostile to the old order, doctrines of human rights, doctrines of the residence of power, new doctrines of authority and of the revolt against authority. The controls man had acquired over nature depended on a belief in law; not the old man-oriented "law of nature," but universal inexorable law, in contrast alike with variant ethical codes and with the violable and forever changing laws of men. Thus a new rationalism arose that spurned the sanctity of prescription and ridiculed the magic of caste.

In the third place, the new industry brought with it a continuous reorganizing of society. It broke down the insulation of groups and of areas. Agriculture, instead of being the occupation of the vast majority of men, became that of an ever lessening minority and was itself transformed in the process. The prestige of landownership was deflated. Large-scale production meant large-scale organization. On the one hand the great corporation came into being—combines, cartels, central banks, financial syndicates, and all the rest. On the other hand there arose the great labor unions and federations of labor. For the first time in history labor became a power, strong enough to deal on equal terms with any other economic power; so

14

much so that in time labor leaders could rebuff kings and presidents or themselves aspire to rule. Thus were exalted the lowly of former days. No longer was there any predestinated ruling class.

Against these invasive changes the old unity, the old trinity of power fought a losing fight. The old unity was dissolved. Two alternatives were now open: a new type of inclusive concentrated power might be set up; or the different forms of social power might reach some kind of interadjustment or equilibrium. It was a question of whether human society should remain "open," free to the play of the creative forces within it, or whether it should again become closed, ruled from above by a close-knit hierarchy of all-inclusive power. In this issue, as we shall see, the relation of economic power to political power plays a most important part.

3

The stripping of the mantle of authority from an entrenched ruling class was a great turning-point in the history of mankind. How crucial it was, how revolutionary it has proved to be, is perhaps less obvious to Americans than to other peoples. As they broke into a new continent where they had to build a new society and to adjust themselves to new conditions and form new habits, the traditions that traveled with them on their ships took shallower roots in the new earth. Above all, the sanctity of landownership, on which rested the historical class structure of the older world, became dissipated in the presence of an expanding frontier that offered free acres to the adventurous. Therefore of all countries the United States has been least threatened by *social* revolution, and still seems least likely to be, unless perhaps atomic warfare brings cataclysms of a kind that have never been known before.

In the greater history of mankind every turning-point has been marked by the successful assault alike on a long-sanctified doctrine of authority and on a long-established social system in which that doctrine was entrenched.

The break-up of the old authority was not a temporary thing that could be reversed by counteraction at a later time. The old class structure was destroyed by industrial and technological change. The distribution of power in society was fundamentally changed. A new class structure of some kind had to take its place. The classless society was a dream of an unknown future, whether the dreamers were Marxist visionaries or American individualists. The new structure might be freer and more flexible, or it might be rigid and hierarchical like the old. It all depended on the new organization of power. One alternative was the democratic structure, in which social class is open and does not carry with it political authority. The avenues of socio-economic advance are not socially—that is, artificially—obstructed. Opinion and initiative are alike free to find expression. The other was the dictatorial structure, in which a new class, no longer the bearers of ancient tradition or descent, concentrates the new techniques of control and of indoctrination to overcome all resistance, turn all dissent into damnable heresy, to establish a new immobility, and to harden into terror-guarded fixity the formula of its power.

A first condition of the dictatorial alternative is a new fusion of economic and political power. It differs from the old fusion in that it is done in the name of the people. This claim, false as it proves to be, is quite necessary, since class is officially abolished and some basis for authority, other than the stark possession of power, must always be promulgated. In the democratic alternative, as it has emerged historically, economic power and political power are not co-ordinated. In other words, there is private economic power. It is of course subject to political controls, but it remains private. Government has some public economic power, together with the comprehensive authority to regulate economic affairs.

The distinction we have just drawn is primary. Governmental regulation of economic affairs, operating in accordance with the movements of public opinion, is an utterly different thing from the fusion of economic and political power. Private economic power, the control of economic resources that was vested in groups outside the circle of government, in groups that were not part of a ruling class, played an essential role in the growth of democracy, as I shall presently show. This private economic power gave a ground for effective resistance to the absolutism of government. The question must then be raised whether that ground of resistance is still needed in the more developed democracies of our own time, whether indeed democracy could survive even today if the role of private economic power were ended.

Modern democracy, the only broad-based kind, the only kind that has shown any enduring quality, came into gradual being as a certain amount of resources, of private economic power, came into the hands of the non-ruling classes. Without these resources the subject classes would have been far more helpless and could hardly have shown the independence and the solidarity that successfully resisted the impositions of government.

The historical role of the middle classes was to bring democracy to birth. The middle classes were those groups who, one way or another, acquired a modicum of economic power. The poorest classes never succeeded in wresting privileges from their rulers. They were capable only of sporadic and short-lived revolt, and that only under the most desperate conditions. Once the middle classes had opened the way, the poorest might share the victory. Always it was the middle classes who broke through the ancient monopoly of power. They did it under the banner of the democratic faith, however narrowly they may have interpreted that faith. It was so in Greece and in Rome, where the middle classes gained resources with the expansion of empire, through trade, through managerial enterprises, though such occupations as tax-farming, and through deals in government contracts. It was so in the "free" cities of the later Middle Ages and the Renaissance, where the merchant and craft guilds grew strong. It was so again in England, where the growing middle classes combined shipbuilding and seafaring and trading with farming. They became strong enough to hold the purse strings of government, as the Stuarts learned to their sorrow. The war-cry of "no taxation without representation" was carried through to victory.

In England it was a slow-developing democracy, the mere beginnings of democracy for a time, but it opened the way for a later age. This growth of democracy was made possible only by the combination of private economic power with a new vision of a free people, the spirit of the democratic faith.

Let us note again what private economic power means. It does not mean *laisser-faire*. It means that a substantial portion of the economic enterprise of a community is in private hands, subject only to the general oversight of government. It means that a substantial portion of the economic decisions of a community is not made by government, either directly or indirectly. It means there are markets for goods and services where the supply and the price are not set by edict. It means there is always an area in which men can make a living and carry on their business without becoming the agents or employees of the state.

Public and Private Economic Power

It was, then, the historical role of private economic power to foster and sustain the rise of democracy. Is that role ended? Is it no longer needed? It will help us to answer that question if we examine more closely the way we have traveled.

II

The Rise of
Private Economic Power

1

IN THE FEUDAL SOCIETY that found its most characteristic form in Europe after the downfall of Rome the ruling class owned all the wealth. Wealth meant landownership, and to own land was to govern land—the little rulers owned a little land and the bigger rulers owned larger domains, up to the feudal sovereign who had the overlordship of it all. In such a society, wherever it remained purely feudal, the subject classes could never acquire any wealth. There was no middle class. There was no movement toward democracy. In feudal society there is no lever for the overthrow of oligarchy. Only outside of its range could a middle class arise.

The opportunity came early in England. It was protected from the invasions that devastated the countries of continental Europe. In its insular seclusion the inherently antifeudal sense of nationality began to emerge. Its trading position brought profits to it and spoils, especially after the discovery of the great continent far to the west. So there developed a middle class of traders, adventurers, shipbuilders, captains, guildsmen, and substantial farmers. Excluded from the monopoly of power, this middle class step by step wrested privileges from the ruling class. It became important enough to have its representatives included in the councils of the realm. This lower house, the Commons, gradually gained prestige and became itself a power. It had its ups and downs until in the seventeenth century a crucial issue was fought out between parliament and king. The middle classes were now important enough to be able to refuse to be taxed without their own consent. It came to a civil war and it culminated in an event that gave an unprecedented shock to the whole tradition of authority, the death of a king of England on the scaffold.

In the course of that struggle there was a remarkable upsurge of democratic doctrines. The violence of the struggle gave new intensity to the faith in which it was fought. Doctrines were proclaimed that had been unsounded for a thousand years and some that had scarcely at all been heard before. There was talk of an Englishman's "birthright," independent of his station. Every man, be he rich or poor, should be free to live his own life. There was talk of a new equality, of the rights of man, of the sovereignty of the people.

There were the radical Levellers and the still more radical Diggers. There were the new constitutionalists, the men of the covenant, the Independents. There were outcries against the union of church and state. Against these new voices the timorous Hobbes set forth his doctrine of Leviathan, the doctrine of total surrender to authority as the only alternative to chaos and ceaseless turmoil. But the times were against him. It was the last desperate stand in England of the old authoritarianism. That cause was lost in the seventeenth century. To defeat it was the great achievement of the English middle classes, the merchants and the traders, the guildsmen and the yeomen.

This was the most convulsive revolution that England has ever known. The political strife was much complicated by ecclesiastical strife. The claim has been made that it was primarily the spirit of religious dissent, demanding freedom of worship against the establishment, that bred the democracy of England. It has been claimed that it was the Puritan congregation, breaking away from hierarchical control, seeking its own autonomy, its freedom to worship God in its own way, that was the model and the exemplar of what democracy meant. It is true that the Puritans and other nonconforming groups resisted the bishops and the ecclesiastical courts, attacked the absolutist union of church and state, and repudiated the doctrine of the divine right of kings. But that is only one side of the story.

In the first place, the religious dissent against the establishment was predominantly a middle-class movement. To it rallied the same elements that fought on the constitutional front, the side of the commons against the monarchy. The whole uprising was a middle-class onslaught against the entrenched order of power. The bishops of the Church of England were deeply committed to the old order. The Puritans and the Presbyterians were attacking the class monopoly of ecclesiastical authority, and ecclesiastical authority was state authority. Certainly the religious attitudes that were evoked in this process had great political significance. They gave a new quality to the democratic faith. They stressed the importance of the individual in the sight of God and thus gave him a new standing as a person, apart from rank or station, regardless of property or wealth. But in the main the religious protest can be regarded, from the political point of view, as one aspect of the middle-class revolt against absolute class-bound authority. It was part of the total attack on the privileges and prerogatives of the ruling class.

This attack came to a head on the economic front. The focus of the struggle was the claim of the monarchy to levy taxes without the consent of the commons. It was on this issue—the commons against the royalists—that the civil war was fought. It was this issue that brought Charles I to trial and execution. It was over this issue that parliament triumphed—no taxation without representation—just as it was this issue that precipitated the American Revolution.

The English middle classes had the independence to resist and the means as well as the will to curb the forces of autocracy. They were in this position because they had acquired a measure of private economic power—private in the sense that it was outside the feudalized union of land-ownership and political authority. Without this means at their disposal they could not have broken the dominance of the ruling class, invested as it was with the ancient attributes of sovereignty. The sources of middle-class wealth had been ignored or despised by the land-conscious aristocracy. In a sense it was their concept of the narrow limits of the occupations befitting the well-born that allowed this new source of power to fall into other hands than theirs. Trade and business enterprise were not honorific occupations. But the means they provided proved to be the wedge that rifted and at length split apart the unity of economic and political power.

It is important to note the particular sense in which the means owned by these middle-class groups constituted *private* economic power. It is not merely that these means were personal possessions, owned distributively and not collectively. The landed estates of the ruling classes had also their personal owners. But landownership as such carried with it an area of political authority, whereas trading wealth did not. Moreover, the estate-owners formed a closed or nearly closed class, exclusively privileged and constituting a hierarchy of power of which the monarch was the apex. Wealth in land had thus a public or political significance. It was the wealth of a ruling class and constituted a basis for its right to rule. The wealth of the merchant or the guildsman or the tenant farmer had no such significance. Until, then, a middle class developed, there was no economic power outside of the ruling class, and the economic controls exercised by the latter were a potent instrument of their authority. In our own times a similar union of political and economic power has been achieved, though in a very different way, in the totalitarian state. There all basic wealth—the means of production—is collectively owned, but since the control over it is in the hands of a ruling class, the "party," the result for the subject classes —for all, that is, who do not belong to the party hierarchy —is pretty much the same as though the ruling class distributively owned all the wealth of the community.

To return to our thesis, the militant middle class of seventeenth-century England grew strong enough to break the monopoly of governing power and gain a share of it for themselves. They may have been less concerned with the principles of democracy than with the assurance of their own interests. Men fight for a good cause from mixed motives, but the cause remains good. And they could not carry on the struggle without raising the banner of democracy, enlisting on their side the forward-looking men who cherished democratic ideals.

2

They won their victory, and the ardor of their faith began to cool. Stability succeeded revolution and an interlude in which England had its one taste of a species of dictatorship. From the time of Locke to the time of Burke democracy became thought of as the rule of the men of property, the comfortable bourgeoisie, the men with a stake in the country. Locke was a major prophet of the eighteenth-century gospel, and for Locke the main purpose of government was to preserve property, large and small. Property was now thought of as private in a very exclusive

24

sense, something privately acquired by a man's own labor and ingenuity, something with which government had nothing directly to do, except to put a legal fence around it. It was a comfortable middle-class doctrine, reflecting the outcome of the first English revolution, and it was a doctrine quite antithetical to that of the old feudal ruling class.

But with this habit of thought the true conception of democracy was dimmed, the conception that had found its way to first articulate expression in the blazing times of the seventeenth century. For democracy must be rooted in the recognition of the worth of personality, of the value and potentiality of the human being, apart from rank and property alike. The Levellers may have been impractical idealists, and certainly they had no respected philosopher to espouse their cause. But they had sensed the full meaning of democracy, that assures to the "poorest he in England" the right to live his life no less than to the "richest he." Whereas the eighteenth-century doctrine made a modicum of property the criterion of citizenship. As Defoe put it, England had substituted for the divine right of kings the divine right of freeholders. If it was an approach to democracy, it became again a diluted form of the ancient doctrine, broadened now to include the middle classes, that joined together authority and property and power.

There was of course a difference. The assault on the old aristocracy had the objective of setting limits to the prerogatives of a ruling class, which meant setting constitutional limits to the power of the executive branch of government. The demand for inviolate rights, for protection against arbitrary decrees, against the intrusion of government into the area of a man's faith and conscience, announced the principle that there were limits to what government could or should do. This principle is of cardinal importance in the doctrine of democracy. There are certain vital concerns of men that are *private,* in the sense that government shall not intrude its coercive arm into them. It becomes the fundamental law that government shall not do so and so, shall not, for example, impose a religious faith on its citizens or subject any citizen to any disability on the ground of his faith. The religious issue played an important role in the establishment of this principle. But, as we have seen, the crucial struggle was waged over an economic issue. In the eighteenth century, however, the economic issue took a very different form. Now the doctrine took hold that government should keep its hands off economic affairs and that practically the whole range of economic activity should be treated as a private area.

This doctrine was a protest against the obsolete regulations that fettered the expansive trade and industry of a changing economy, against the rusty contrivances of the mercantilists to secure a "balance of trade," against such anachronistic ordinances as the statute of apprentices. So far it was a salutary protest. But it did not stop there. It was not content with the removal of old restrictions, it repudiated practically all controls of any kind. "Whate'er is least administered is best." It discovered that, when government withdraws, the economic system has a beautiful self-regulating mechanism. This automatic regulation is vastly superior to any governmental regulation, for it gives every man what he deserves to get and prevents any man from getting more than a fair return. It keeps everything at its proper level, prices and wages and profits, and when some conjuncture or accident disturbs this level it restores again the true equilibrium.

As so often happens, an idea with a core of wisdom in it was thus grossly exaggerated into a total theory of government. This eighteenth-century liberalism became in effect identified with the meaning of democracy. It had most unhappy consequences when the new industries of the Industrial Revolution began their unregulated course.

Now was the low tide of modern democracy. It had become a doctrine of inertia, lacking all robustness of principle, a complacent doctrine that hugged the delusion that all was well with the world if only government would leave it alone. It claimed to vindicate the liberty of the individual, but it refused to comprehend the fact that economic power can be as coercive and as cruel as political power. It was against bureaucratic interference but it closed its eyes to private exploitation. New men of power rose from the middle classes, and sometimes from the working classes too, who gained control of the new economic forces to serve their own ends and were only too happy that government should leave them alone.

Liberalism became a flaccid substitute for democracy, closing its eyes to what was happening in the textile factories and in the mines—what was happening to the men and women and children who were increasingly drawn into the industrial vortex, where inordinate hours and evil conditions and under-subsistence wages and unprotected machinery and a pervading sense of insecurity and oppression sapped the life and health and morale of the new working class.

Here was the complete reversal of an older concept. Here was the proclamation of the total separation of economics from politics, of economic power from political power. In the ancient view all economic power was public power. In the new liberalism all economic power should be, with meager limitations for the sake of national defense, private power, controlled not by government but by an overruling harmony, an all-wise Providence. The old doctrine made democracy unattainable. The new doctrine made it merely impotent.

The democratic faith needed to be reborn. It had to

regain, for the industrial era, the conviction that the final objective was not the liberation of the economic arena but the liberation of the human being; and that the business of government was to do what it could do to achieve that end, and ,to refrain from doing what interferes with or cramps the attainment of that end.

3

The new impulse came from France. Rousseau was its ambiguous prophet, and its fiery manifestation was the French Revolution. For Rousseau the people were the state, the people as persons in community, without distinction of class or wealth or race. These differences should have no political significance; all rights belonged to men as men. The state is the creation of their common will to belong together, and only in that union of wills and hearts can man find alike freedom and fulfillment.

Here was a complete repudiation of all the barriers within which the spirit of democracy had been confined. It sounded a new age. But Rousseau unhappily combined his doctrine of the people and its sovereignty with false and mystical notions of an organic will, a will of the whole beyond the will of majorities and minorities, beyond parties and politics—an insidious and beguiling concept that strangely led the prophet of democracy to the verge of totalitarianism. It is the same false gospel that today allows Soviet Russia to talk of the people's state, when all it means is the puppet state pulled by the strings of the communist operator.

But the notion of democracy, heralded so ambivalently by Rousseau, was stirring in the peoples. It was responsive to the spirit of nationalism, the growing sense of the inclusive folk. It was developed in protest against the inse-

curities and hazards and exploitations of the new industry. While the nineteenth century was a time of great
economic expansion, of unprecedented new wealth, and of
relative peace—in the shelter of which the middle classes
became ever larger and more dominant and more comfortable—there was a new unrest fermenting underneath
its prosperity. The harvest of a period of uncontrolled industrialism was being reaped. On the one hand there was
a sense of homelessness, of insecurity, of the oppressiveness
of economic subjection, and on the other hand a realization
of the potentialities of a new instrument that might change
it all. This was the power of organization; the working
classes were becoming conscious that in the organization of
labor they had a new and formidable kind of private economic power. Labor organization, supplemented by the
labor vote, at first slowly, then with increasing momentum,
grew into one of the great agencies that put strong pressure
on government to make it serve their interests.

One result of this and other new conditions was a re-
orientation of the functions of the state. It became increasingly accepted that the business of government included
the protection of the people against the consequences of
the hazards of an industrial society, against penury and
unemployment, against preventable ill-health, against in-
sanitary and overcongested housing, against the economic
insecurity of old age. On the positive side the conception
took hold that there was a minimum standard of healthful
and decent living that, in this age of greater abundance,
should be assured to all citizens for the greater welfare of
the whole. This is the conception of the "welfare state." Its
significance for the present time is so great that we must
pause to dwell on it.

There is a common confusion, sedulously propagated
from certain quarters in the United States, that the welfare

state and the socialist state are indistinguishable in kind. Welfare measures are bitterly opposed on the ground that they are socialistic or even communistic. But the distinction between the two is perfectly simple. In the welfare state the goal is the adequate provision of protection against want and insecurity and the safeguarding of the health and the general well-being of the people. All modern states are increasingly welfare states. The trend in that direction is irresistible. Therefore it is particularly unwise to identify it with the coming of communism. If we do not welcome it as the most fundamental of all economies we should at least recognize in it the surest protection against the peril of communist infiltration.

Why are men susceptible to communist propaganda? There are some who through personal frustrations or a quirk of disposition become psychopathically hostile to the society in which they live. But the majority, the rank and file who march under the red banner, do so because they crave any refuge, any promised deliverance, from haunting economic insecurity, from the strains and buffets of the struggle to keep their heads above the economic waters. Give them economic security, give them a reasonable opportunity to make their way to safety, and their ears will be deaf to the Soviet siren voices.

The welfare state and the socialist state are quite different affairs—and the communist state in turn is a very particular kind of socialist state. It is essential to make these elementary distinctions. The welfare state is consistent with private economic power. The socialist state is by definition opposed to it. It would convert private economic power back into public power.

It was in the nineteenth century that the Industrial Revolution first revealed its character, and in doing so exposed at once the need and the opportunity for the welfare state. Vast changes took place as the century advanced

30

—the increasing mechanization of the productive apparatus, the increasing division of labor, the increasing competitiveness of business and the consequent movements for monopoly controls, the development of great cyclical fluctuations in business activity, bringing sudden changes in the volume of employment and in price levels, and with all that the increasing insecurity and economic detachment of the worker's life, even though in good times he attained a standard of living never achieved before. At the same time there was a vast increase in the sum total of wealth and in the size of the population. It was a century of discovery and invention, a century of growing prosperity for those who were in a position to be in on it, and a century of peace. The period from 1815 to 1914 was at once the most prosperous and the most peaceful the Western World had known.

It was a century of optimism, even of utopian dreams. It was a century in which democracy expanded, spreading to new countries, so that to many democracy and civilization seemed to be inseparable companions. It was a century in which the middle classes increased and gained new power. Nevertheless there were signs that this time of accelerated prosperity nourished some deep-working evil hidden from the optimists who hailed the inevitable march of progress.

The new conditions of work, the new routines, the new mechanizations, the new organizations were fostering underneath the surface a sense of instability and displacement. Men were losing their social anchorage, their anchorage in the life of the neighborhood and the community. There was a loosening of the social bond, frayed by the mobility, the competitiveness, and the impersonality of the changeful urban environment. The framework of living was shaken. There was little to replace the traditions that bound men together in the smaller communities of former days. The times were more bounteous but there was restlessness and homelessness below the middle-class complacency.

4

These underground currents may help to explain a curious phenomenon. The century from the end of the Napoleonic Wars to the outbreak of the First World War was notable for the unwonted reign of peace, until in the more sheltered countries men began to think of war as a thing of the past. Nevertheless this century bred more deep-biting doctrines of strife and division than any previous time had registered. Above there was the smoothness of upper-class conservatism and middle-class morality, the pride of national greatness, the belief in eternal progress—

> *God's in his heaven:*
> *All's right with the world—*

but below there were stirring new discordant myths, mightily disturbing heresies.

It was the century of Darwin, whose followers made incessant struggle and internecine destruction the very law of life. It was the century of Marx, to whom all human history was little more than the record of class war, which could end only by the violent overthrow of one class by the other. It was at the end the century of Freud, who carried the thesis of conflict into the heart of love itself and discovered the roots of undying strife in the infant sucking at his mother's breast. And there were besides the racialists, men like Lapouge and Gobineau, who inspired the doctrine Hitler at length inherited. There were the ultranationalists and the militarists, who in a blunter way made war the medicine of mankind. There were the amoralists, such as Treitzschke. The doctrines of all these, widely divergent as they were, were all doctrines of pitiless strife,

strife rooted in the very nature of things. They made the dividing sword the supreme arbiter of human society.

We think of the nineteenth century as the comfortable age, the Victorian age. Why was it also the seedtime of these deep-cleaving doctrines? Doctrines that derided the notion of humanity, despised democracy, belittled the common, the universal, in man, and championed the necessity and the supremacy of incessant war, in which the strong-willed, the aggressive, as individual, as superman, as group, as nation, as race, annihilated the weaker members or made them the servants of their own ruthless dominance.

Bred in a century of peace between two eras of war, these doctrines have come to fruition in this century of ours, bringing waves of overwhelming destruction over the earth.

It is tempting to speculate why they should have been formulated in that time of peace. The characterizations we so easily give to periods of history may often be superficial. What they incubate may be more significant than what is proclaimed from the rostrum or in the editorial columns. Were these doctrines the fruits of revulsion from the mechanization and rationalization of the new industrial age? Were they the offspring of a new insecurity, both social and economic? Were they due to the loss of tradition and the rejection of any ground of authority in a more skeptical and sophisticated world? Was there in consequence a loss of the sense of community, of belongingness? Did all these conditions conspire to weaken the social bond, so that doctrines of sheer divisiveness found a new appeal? Were the new dogmas a substitute for the loss of authority, and the new fierce insistence on partial or mythical unities —the class, the party, the elite, the race—a compensation for the rejection of a more integral solidarity?

We leave these intriguing speculations aside. Our theme leads elsewhere. We are particularly concerned with one

33

of these doctrines of division, the doctrine that in our days has become vastly more formidable than all the rest. The economic challenge to democracy found its sharpest expression in Karl Marx. His doctrine, like that of the later totalitarians, was one of wrathful division. He divided because he wanted to eliminate one of the two things thus opposed, in order to proclaim a new social unity constituted solely of the other. Foremost of the things he would eliminate was private economic power.

To assess the deadly challenge to democracy therein contained I ask the indulgence of the reader if we examine anew the significance of this much-examined doctrine.

III

The Portent of Karl Marx

1

THE FIRST really great manifestation of private economic power came with the rise of modern industry and the growth of industrial capitalism. In previous periods the only way in which any private economic power could arise was in the pursuit of occupations neglected or despised by the ruling class. Thus in Rome, for example, the occupation of tax-farming was relegated to a sort of middle class, the so-called "knights" or horsemen, and when with the expansion of Roman territories it became a lucrative and large-scale business, this class in turn gained political status. Again, in the Middle Ages, with the church ban on "usury," finance capital was acquired by groups debarred from more honorific occupations, including notably some Jewish bankers. Trading had always been regarded as a lower-class occupation, and we have seen how in England, because of its trading facilities and other advantages, the middle classes had made more headway than elsewhere. But before the Industrial Revolution, while they were able to curb the privileges and powers of the old ruling class and establish a measure of democracy, they were not yet in the seats of power.

The new industry was developed by the middle classes. Now for the first time the men of the people had a great opportunity to become masters of the situation. The new wealth, unlike landed wealth, had a remarkable capacity for multiplying itself. It began to challenge landed wealth and at length to conquer it. The middle classes rose to full power. The landed classes began to marry into industrial wealth. Their reign was coming to an end. For the first time the preponderance of economic power fell into private hands, in the sense that it was dissociated from the processes of government. It became strong enough to determine, from the outside as it were, the policies of government. At first its main interest was to prevent government from interfering with its operations. This is what *laisser-faire* meant.

Now this new industrial capitalism was hideously short-sighted, even in its own interest. Selfish interests are often stupid and they do great harm only because they are stupid as well as selfish. The new industry changed everything it touched—the way of work, the way of life, the way of association, the habits of body and mind. There was crying need for regulation, as there always is when an old system is dethroned. But the gospel of industrial capitalism was: hands off! It blindly maintained the doctrine, delivered by Adam Smith before the new factories and the mines had begun to operate, that the economic order is beautifully self-regulating. This faith was so congenial to those who saw a new avenue of wealth opening before their unaccustomed eyes that they were oblivious of the devastation of the countryside, of the misery of the wages they paid, of the effect on children and on women of twelve-hour days in unhealthy mines and unprotected factories, of the total dissolution of healthy human relationships. Never did a group of power-holders show less foresight, less comprehension, less humanity than did the first capitalists of the coal mines and the textile mills.

There were machine-smashing riots and other ineffective protests. Strange new doctrines began to be heard, the first wave of socialist theories heralding the deeper commotions that were to come. The earlier socialists of the nine-

36

teenth century were men of little influence, visionaries and rebels with little grasp of the practicable. There was a rare exception in Robert Owen, who went so far as to set up a model village for an industrial society. But it was not until the middle of the nineteenth century that any socialist doctrine was developed with sufficient robustness to be a potential threat to the new era of capitalism. In 1848 Marx and Engels gave to the world the *Communist Manifesto*.

The Marxist doctrine derived its inspiration from the French Revolution, and its particular dogmatism from the metaphysics of Hegel. Its chief author was a man who was at war with society. His animus was not originally directed against capitalism at all. He cherished a deep resentment against all those in power, against all constituted authority. He was a man of the middle classes, who nourished a special source of embitterment. He never suffered the hardships of factory or mine. He knew nothing about these things until later on he began to study in the British Museum. He scarcely ever met a "proletarian," and when at length, as the leader of a movement, he met some of the proletarian leaders he soon quarreled with them.

It was another kind of resentment that rankled in him. Son of a well-to-do Jewish lawyer in a Prussian town, he was a bright, quick-thoughted child who realized all too soon that his people were a people apart, victims of an ancient self-perpetuating prejudice. Soon after his birth his father, descendant of a line of rabbis, deserted his tradition and joined the Protestant evangelical church. There can be little doubt that he was prompted by social considerations—he was the legal agent of the local nobility and on good terms with them. Whatever the motivation, there were some unhappy consequences. His mother refused, for a number of years—the years of Karl's childhood— to go along with his father. There was tension in the home. No doubt the impact on the sensitive child was profound.

It probably explains, among other things, the aversion he early manifested to all religions. It planted no doubt the deep lonely disquietude that later, when he had suffered various rebuffs, flared into fierce embitterment and a violent animosity against the whole order of things. He needed a new drastic triumphant dogma that would vindicate him against the world. Later on he found it in communism, to which he was led by the "communist rabbi," Moses Hess. He saw in it, with its doctrine of class war and final revolution, a powerful instrument for the overthrow of the social order. He himself called it "the material weapon of philosophy." He sharpened the weapon with great skill and endless energy. He envenomed its edge.

There is something here that is well worth reflecting on. The leading spirits of communism—in countries, that is, where it is not already enthroned—have espoused it not because of a detestation of capitalism but because for one reason or another they are at war with the society in which they live. It was so again with Lenin, son of a school inspector who lived in a provincial town on the Volga. What did he know or care about capitalism in a region and in a country where feudalism prevailed? He was still a schoolboy when his older brother was executed for conspiring in a plot against the Czar, filling him with implacable hatred of the establishment. His fiery spirit soon found in the principles of international communism the most potent gospel for the destruction of all he hated.

What is true of the leaders is true of many in the lower echelons. Some are simply natural rebels, though they usually tone down in later years. Some are disgruntled seekers after power, who see no other way to attain it. Some are victims of social prejudice or economic discrimination. These tend to be the most inflexible and extreme. Members of socially and economically disprivileged minority groups join the party in disproportionate numbers. In a word, it is our own betrayal of democracy more than the shortcomings of capitalism that fills the communist ranks. Nothing embitters the heart of a man like the brand of inferiority. Treat men squarely as fellow men, whatever be their race or color or religion, do not fasten on any groups the stigma of alienhood or inferiority—and in a country like ours communism will shrink to nothingness.

The leaders of a communist movement are most likely to be power-hungry persons; the followers are mainly people who are disoriented and starving for lack of security. It may be economic insecurity, but frequently it is social insecurity, status insecurity, such as rankles in the minds of the victims of prejudice. Here may be the explanation of a further fact that is seldom noted. Many of the most devout and most inflexible converts to the party are women. In most cases I have known personally, where a husband and wife have both taken up communism or at least displayed definite communist sympathies, the wife has been the driving and sustaining force. Women have generally more reason than men to be concerned, from an early age, with the problem of social status. For most women status and security must be sought through marriage. This condition is inherent in our social order and is historically associated with an assumption of inferiority, an assumption that is conveyed by various usages and conventions of society. The young man seeks social security by becoming economically self-sustaining, the young woman most often by acquiring the man's economic support in marriage. The reckoning that attaches inferiority to this difference is of course intrinsically false, since the woman's contribution in the marital relationship is at least as primary as that of the man. But in a civilization dominated by a money economy the assumption is prevalent. Against the assumption it is natural that women of high spirit should rebel. Given a certain conjuncture of aggravating conditions, their protest may make them more sympathetic to communism, which among its specious promises has offered them, since the time of the *Communist Manifesto,* deliverance from economic dependence.

Karl Marx, himself highly sensitive to imputations of social inferiority, found it convenient to identify the root of all evil, including social insecurity, with the economic order. He was acutely aware, on the one hand, of the power that lay in organization and, on the other, of the weak points of nineteenth-century capitalism. If the worker was a mere replaceable unit in a production line, performing mechanical operations that meant nothing to him, for the greater profit of a boss who hired and fired him at will, if a man's livelihood was at the mercy of a fluctuating market and there was no security anywhere, then there must be underneath a smoldering volume of unrest and discontent that could be roused and marshaled under the red banner. While Marx and Engels were preparing the *Communist Manifesto* a whole series of revolutions were brewing in continental Europe, coming to a climax in the year 1848. The time seemed ripe. The traditions of authority were being weakened and the distribution of power, both political and economic, was changing in a way that seemed favorable to the new gospel. Marx was not only the prophet of communism but also the skillful engineer of revolution. The fall of capitalism was, according to the creed, inevitable—but it might as well be hastened.

The appeal of his doctrine lay not merely in his exposure of the weaknesses of capitalism but in his cocksure falsifications of part truths into a final revelation of the whole history of human society, in his utter simplification of human nature and of the causes of things into a framework for an all-sufficient dogma, in his "scientific" prediction of a day of judgment on which, by inevitable law, capitalistic society must perish and the "workers" rule the world.

His economics was fallacious, his so-called dialectic was completely regardless of the history it professed to interpret, his materialism was a mere upside-down version of the pretentious Hegelian philosophy he was taught at college, and his predictions nearly all went wrong. But he offered a fighting faith to those who felt exploited or oppressed or despised or slighted, and he gave them boundless assurances of victory.

To Marx economic power is the basis, the condition, of all social power. The power of government is merely the instrument of economic power. The importance of economic power in man's history had been neglected prior to Marx and there was enough truth in his doctrine to make it very plausible, though as always Marx reduced the record to his own black-and-white. For Marx the institutions of government are nothing but a device contrived by the possessors of economic power to exploit and regiment the people. The main force in history is class war. Every historical system has in it the seeds of its own decay. Class struggle is the agency by which it is overthrown and replaced by its opposite, its "antithesis." So it is with "capitalist society." The seeds of its dissolution are already ripened.

We are not concerned with an exposition of Marxism, with its endless interpretations and reinterpretations, with the new direction it was given by Lenin, or with its final sanctification under Stalin. What concerns us is its meaning on the economic front and its menace for democracy— for all democracy and for every attribute and endeavor and goal associated with it.

2

Marxism is not only a threat; it is also a challenge to democracy. And if we meet the challenge we need not fear the threat.

Democracy and the Economic Challenge

The challenge comes on the socio-economic front. The early period of industrial capitalism left a bitter memory and a dangerous legacy. Gradually regulative forces have reformed its major evils, but in various countries enough still remain to make the appeal of communism still formidable, especially in times of crisis. Communism came with a promise of release from the malaise of industrial capitalism, from its insecurities, from the exposed economic detachment of the industrial worker, the clerk, the small-time dealer, the multitude who have no substantial reserves, no promise in their future, no assurance against continued unemployment or against an old age of dependency. Communism, like other types of socialism, removes this economic specter. The more prosperous classes do not appreciate what this specter threatens, do not realize how it haunts and invades the mind, nor how much those who sense it would surrender to have the assurance that it was banned forever.

Communism gives the assurance and falsely tells them they would surrender nothing. It does not mention the price—regimentation and terrorism and ruthless control over life and thought. But those who have felt the power of the specter do not reckon, do not comprehend, the price. That is why, in countries where crisis after crisis has intensified economic insecurity—in Italy and in France and previously in Germany, in the impoverished and war-swept areas of the Orient—so many thousands have joined the communist ranks. To the average man the idea of liberty seems remote from the worries of everyday existence, whereas the sense of insecurity grows greater as the years go by.

Here, then, is the communist challenge to democracy. It is the challenge to democracy, and not that to capitalism, with which we are here concerned. The relation of democracy to capitalism is a matter we shall take up later.

42

The Portent of Karl Marx

The communists wish democracy no good, but their challenge can do it a great service if they stimulate democracy to remove its most serious weakness, so that its gift of liberty is no longer associated with needless insecurity. Already, before the challenge, democracy had gone some way in this direction. But some democratic countries, and not least our own, still fail to provide for many of their citizens the access to opportunities without which political liberties seem empty privileges, or the safeguards against economic hazards without which they cannot appreciate constitutional rights. Democracy by giving these assurances will vindicate its faith in the human being as primary value, while still retaining the only way of government that allows men to work out their own salvation and thus liberates the creative achievements of the free community.

Communism slanders democracy at every point, but its effective attack is at the point of weakness, the lack of economic security. And yet this lack cannot properly be called a weakness of democracy itself but only of particular democratic societies. The democratic system of government is in no sense inconsistent with the provision of a reasonable security. To provide it, a democracy has only to ask for it. It depends on public opinion, not on the democratic structure. In various democracies the provision has already been made; in the others it is in part available. The weakness attacked by communism is therefore at worst a curable one. But the weakness of communism itself is incurable. There is a lie in its soul that is eating out the faith of its devotees and leaving only the bare ribs of power. Communism, so called, Sovietism, Marxism, is not and can never be a *communist* system. It is a peculiarly rigid form of state capitalism controlled by an elite.

The means communism must use forever defeats the end it proclaims. It professes to establish the reign of liberty by converting, forcefully, all private economic power into

43

public economic power, thereby creating the most terrifying engine of power the world has known. The lie eats deeper as the defeat of the end becomes more apparent. The end, the communists declare, is the liberation of the peoples, and the irony grows as they proceed from the "liberation" of their own people to the salvation of the Poles, the Czechs, the Rumanians, the Bulgarians, the Albanians, the Manchurians, the Koreans.

It is never a dictatorship of the proletariat, which is an impossibility; it is always only a dictatorship. The doctrine is equal opportunity and the prospect of a time when each receives according to his needs and gives according to his abilities. The fact is extreme inequality of wealth and great inequality of opportunity. For inequality of power is inequality in all things. Inequality of power is inequality of control over means, and control over means is wealth. It makes no difference that the elite ride in the people's limousines and eat their banquets in the halls of the people. It is still the elite who ride and the people who have their meager rations. The elite travel where they please, and the people whom they serve cannot journey to the next town without a permit.

Here, then, is a remarkable example of the restoration of the ancient trinity of class and property and power. But it is more than a restoration, for the union of the three is more strongly buttressed than in the older oligarchies.

The people own everything, they say, but the people are in effect slaves. The rulers own nothing, they say, but the rulers are masters of everything. That is the lie in the soul of communism. It has destroyed the faith of communism in all whose minds are pervious to the truth.

To understand the character of Marxist communism, and in particular to distinguish it from other forms of socialism, we must remember that this ironclad system was devised by men of powerful minds and powerful purposes

44

who were not in the first place the enemies of an economic system or moved by any sympathies for the working classes, whom they lumped together as the proletariat. Their final objective was not to establish a new and better economic order. Had it been so, they would have set about it in an entirely different way. The founders and leaders of communism were men so embittered against the society in which they lived that they had no allegiance to anything except a visionary belief that if the entire social order were smashed, all the things they hated would disappear along with it. They had no positive vision of a new society—at best a thin mirage of a utopian world without any government at all. They saw it only in negatives; it was classless and stateless. *They had no sense of community.* For Karl Marx community was narrowed to a class that had the function of destroying all other classes. About what would happen thereafter he did not trouble himself overmuch. All his emphasis is turned to the destruction of the existing order. He wrote only a few vague lines about the empty "reign of freedom" that would follow.

To cover this irremediable weakness these vague lines, with additions from Engels, were blown up into big myths, and there has been much disputation about the "withering of the state" and the way in which the classless society would come into being. But these are dead myths, as remote from any possible reality as the average man's idea of paradise. The living myths are made of different stuff. There are the myths that consolidate power, the myths of the infallible leader and the sacrosanct party and the monolithic state, together with the revelation of final truth in the New Testament of communism, Stalin's *Short History of the All-Union Communist Party (Bolshevist)*.

The myths of freedom are set or setting; the myths of power are in the ascendant. What remains are a series of dogmas, a system of techniques skillfully contrived to play

45

on the fears and the hopes of the masses, an elaborate network of controls, secret and open, a corps of experts carefully trained to infiltrate into strategic positions in countries where the All-Union Communist Party (Bolshevist) has no sway. No longer is it the vision of a new earth that captivates these more trusted comrades. Now it is the propulsion of power and the promise of power. It is a simpler delusion, but most often, for them, it is a delusion still. For the upper servants of absolute power are as much the slaves of their masters as are the rest, except that their position is less secure, for if they should be found wanting on any score the end is oblivion—or liquidation.

3

So far we have been considering one particular system that has restored the unity of economic power and political power. It has done so on the ground of doctrines that have no inherent relation to the principle of socialism—for reasons I have already suggested. It was born in hatred and bred in violence. It sought a way of power that would be irresistible for its purposes. Therefore it set itself to work up enough resentment against the weaknesses of capitalism to enable it to win the supreme control that the abolition of private economic power would put in its hands.

Communism, however, is only one of the forms of socialism. The nineteenth century gave birth to many forms. All of them had the same immediate objective: the abolition of private economic power. Most of them were based on a genuine conviction that a collectivistic order of society would bring about a great advance in human well-being. Some of them believed in a gradual advance to the goal; others thought of a total all-at-once conversion of the economy. Some of them thought the road lay through increasing experiments in co-operatives; others through legislative socialization of capitalistic industries. Some assigned the new economic functions to the state; others assigned them to special guilds or syndicates. Throughout the nineteenth century a whole array of socialist doctrines came into being, highly divergent in character and most of them very different from the Marxist type.

These doctrines were a natural—indeed, an inevitable —response to the manifested evils of the early unregulated industrialism. The new industrialists abjured, for a long time successfully, any regulation whatever of the formidable new power they possessed. On the one hand they claimed that regulation was unnecessary; on the other they charged that it would be ruinous. The weight of respectable economic theory was all on their side. But the facts were more convincing than the arguments of the Ricardians and of the new men of power. Investigations of the situation began to be made and revealed the most deplorable conditions. Socialistic doctrines arose in protest. Since the new private economic power, as yet untrammeled by effective regulation or by strong trade unions, was responsible, the remedy, according to the socialists, must be the complete abolition of this power.

The modern domination of Marxism has tended to obscure the fact that other forms of socialism have a very different approach. Most of them are free from the venom characteristic of Marxism, especially of its more recent developments. They have been willing to work in constitutional ways. They have been willing to accept partial victories. They have sought to carry the people with them, not to engineer coups, instill hatreds, and crush by violence all opposition. Various types of socialism accept the principle of democracy.

Here comes the crucial question. Can socialism, fully realized, and democracy live together? Can essential freedoms abide in a socialist society? Are those socialists well guided

who believe in democracy and anticipate that, if their objective were reached, a greater democracy would be in-
augurated at the same time? Is a wedding of the two a
reasonable expectation, or would an early divorce be inevitable, in which democracy would be cast out of doors?

We must be careful how we set the question. Is present-
day England a socialist state? It has nationalized some important industries, but no fair-minded observer would dis-
pute the fact that it is still one of the greatest democracies.
And what of Sweden and Denmark and other countries that
follow the middle way? Socialism is not like communism,
a matter of all or nothing. It can exist in any degree. It
always does exist, in every state, in some degree. Every
state, modern or ancient, oligarchical or democratic, ex-
hibits some aspects of socialism. In recent times the degree
has increased considerably in many states. Some at least of
the increase has been the response to a demand, not to an
ideal, the pressure of a situation and not the impulsion of
a theory. All political parties have in different respects
supported the process, although with much controversy
between them concerning the less or the more, the method
and the means.

The complex network of modern technological development has inevitably thrust these problems on government.
Every element of the economy, small or great, becomes
more interdependent with every other, and a blockage anywhere can throw the whole machinery out of gear. Every
new invention, every improvement of technique, creates a
problem of regulation. Consider, for example, what would
be the consequence of the exploitation of radio or television if government did not supervise the allotment of
the channels and the broad conditions of utilization. What
we call capitalism itself would go to pieces did government
not establish principles of order, rules of contract, monetary standards, banking and credit controls, safeguards

48

against misrepresentation, protective measures against unfair competition, and so forth.

No modern economy, no system of "free enterprise," can be fully self-regulating. It is threatened by monopolistic tendencies, the excessive domination of great corporate bodies and combinations. In its attempts to curb these tendencies the government of the United States has undertaken more regulation than the more socialistic government of England. Again, the economy is endangered by the irregularly periodic ups and downs of business, by the inflationary momentum that accompanies the upsurge and the deflationary tendencies of the downward movement, by the crises that culminate from time to time, precipitating large-scale unemployment and the bankruptcy of many businesses. Government is inevitably called on to do something, and if it cannot halt the downward process it must at least do something about the consequences. Again, competitive economic exploitation has proved to be spendthrift or wholly destructive of natural resources— of the soil, the forests, the oil fields, the fisheries, and so on —and to stay this irreparable loss governmental controls must sooner or later be invoked.

For these reasons all modern countries are to a greater or less extent socialistic. It is therefore merely question-begging and prejudice-arousing to denounce any specific proposal assigning a new activity to government as "socialism," instead of discussing it on its merits. It is curious how men who in their business or profession have learned to make distinctions, nicely to calculate the less and the more and to strike a balance, so often disregard the lesson when it comes to political affairs and treat the affairs of the nation with a childish insistence on an "either-or" that would be fatal to their success in any other field.

Just as the word "socialism" is abused in our own controversies, so the word "capitalism" as used by communists has an entirely misleading connotation. Every modern state is socio-capitalistic—a combination of private and public economic power. The "capitalism" of communist propaganda is a grotesque example of the "either-or." Its undiluted "capitalism" is a pure fantasy.

Our question, however, is whether a thoroughgoing socialism—a socialism that nationalizes all the major forms of production, distribution, and exchange—is compatible with a democratic order. The broad tendency of modern times has been to increase the functions of government. How far can the tendency go—can it travel the whole road to the abolition of private economic power—without doing deadly injury to the democratic process? Total socialism means an economy planned, directed, and regulated from the center, organizing the whole economic life, substituting for the play of economic forces four- or five- or ten-year plans. Total socialism means the end of private economic power.

The question then arises whether democracy—any form of genuine democracy—can live together with total economic planning. It is of momentous importance that we should discover and take to heart whatever may be the true answer to this question. Can a way be found of reconciling the two or are they inherently incompatible? Specifically, is it possible to maintain democracy if and when, once more, all private economic power has been converted into public economic power?

IV

Democracy and the Planned Economy

1

THE QUESTION is whether a fully planned, centrally directed economy, which by hypothesis must be a thoroughly socialized economy, can coexist with the attitudes and the processes of democracy.

We have seen that in old-style oligarchies, as in modern dictatorships, all economic power is actually in effect public power. It is power exercised and controlled either directly by government or by a demarcated ruling class so that the distribution of political authority is closely correlated with property holdings. In this respect there is no essential difference between the power of, say, Peter the Great and the power of Stalin—or, if you prefer, between the ruling class of which Stalin and the Politburo form the apex and the ruling class of which Peter and his associates formed the apex. Stalin commands more wealth more absolutely than ever Peter did. Stalin uses the economic resources of Russia to serve his objectives more fully than ever Peter could. And if you say that Stalin holds economic power because he holds political power, while Peter held political power because he held economic power, you are making a highly precarious distinction. Even if it were accurate it would not affect the quality or the exercise of power.

51

We have seen that wherever democracy has appeared, breaking through the entrenchments of a ruling class, whatever other conditions may have favored it there was always the fact that groups outside of the hierarchy had come into possession of some private economic power. It was so in Greece, in Rome, in the free cities of the later medieval world, in pre-industrial England.

We have seen also that democracy in its fuller extension is a very modern development, that so far it has been manifested only in certain industrialized countries of the West and in a few other countries which have inherited the same traditions, and that a primary condition of its advance in these countries was the greatly increased private economic power that came into the hands of an enlarged middle class. Particularly in countries where some degree of democracy already existed this access of economic power, including the power of economic organization, broke down the bulwarks of class privilege and at length made it possible for all classes to enjoy equal political rights and the same fundamental liberties.

We should note in passing that private economic power is by nature and of necessity decentralized. While it may be very unevenly distributed, it can exist only where competition is alive and where every economic interest faces a counterinterest. Where economic power holds any kind of monopoly position, it loses its private character and assumes a political aspect. If it ever were to become a total monopoly, so that within its territory it had no rivals or competitors, did not need to bargain for supplies or to compete for markets or to contend against substitutes for its products, it would become, as it were, a minor government on its own, an *imperium in imperio*. The nearer it approaches to this position, the more need there is for drastic regulation by the state. But our point here is that private economic power retains its private quality and can render the service it has performed in the history of democracy only if it operates from many separate foci within the economy, in such wise that the expansion of each economic power-union always meets the active resistance of others.

Private economic power is private only so far as it is detached from any governmental system and so far as it is unable to carry on any kind of governmental function, overt or disguised. It was only as private economic power became thus detached that it contributed so much to the breaking up of the old oligarchies. It was only thus that it provided a basis of resistance on the part of hitherto subject classes and gave democracy the opportunity to be born.

So we reach the question whether that service is needed any more. It is of course possible that a condition necessary for the rise of a system may be no longer necessary when the system is fully established. It is conceivable that after men have become habituated to democracy and have learned to enjoy its benefits they may not need to retain the weapons with which they fought to win it.

Indeed, it is maintained by thoroughgoing socialists that the sole really or fully democratic system is a collectivist one. They say that unless the people as a unity own the means of production they are not free from political chains. Private economic power is exploitative, inequitable, socially wasteful. Sometimes they say that without collectivism you cannot have "economic democracy" and that this elusive and undefined species is more important than "political democracy."

Thoroughgoing socialism is a doctrine of the reattachment of all economic power to the state authority. It differs from the older attachment in that socialism thus understood identifies the state with the whole people. Now the people and not a ruling class will control. Therefore, they would maintain, if they accept our previous argument, the fact that private economic power was once a condition of democratic advance has now no relevance.

They go further, proclaiming that democracy is in grave danger. Society, as one of them recently put it, is disintegrating before our eyes, and only a fully socialized economy can save it. We are "at the crossroads of history," and only through planning, inclusive planning by a central government, "can catastrophe be avoided." We must "plan for freedom," said Karl Mannheim in his posthumous book, *Freedom, Power, and Democratic Planning.* Other writers warn us that "it is later than you think," and Harold Laski wrote a series of works to show that democracy was "in crisis" and had to choose between full socialism and extinction.

The arguments on which this plea rests are mainly of three kinds. One is that capitalism puts an increasing concentration of wealth and power into the hands of a small elite: those who head the great industrial corporations, the international cartels, the banking syndicates, and an entity known as "Wall Street." The gross disparity of power they wield makes our democracy only a façade for a plutocracy that at any moment may resort to fascism if its power is threatened.

A second argument is that the capitalistic system is proving increasingly incapable of meeting the conditions and needs of modern civilization. The recurrent crises of the "business cycle" are evidences of its incapacity. Modern technology creates an elaborate mechanism of interdependence. A failure or inadequacy anywhere can throw the whole system out of gear. Breakdowns are inevitable without over-all planning. Otherwise there is a drift to chaos.

The third argument claims that the prospective breakdown is not only economic but also moral and social. Indeed, we are already, according to its proponents, in a state of social disintegration. The capitalism system with its competitive detachment of every unit from every other, with its heartlessness, has undermined the moral foundations of society. It has destroyed man's essential loyalties, his sense of community. It breeds what the French call *anomie,* a total loosening of the social bond.

The advocates of a social order that nowhere exists have one great advantage in argument over those who may doubt the prescription. They can point ahead to a land of promise, flowing with milk and honey, the happy fields where peace prevails and brotherly love abounds. They can make it the shining foil against which they draw, with whatever exaggerations they please, lurid pictures of our present discontents. It is an advantage that the communists once possessed and possess no more.

The trouble is that the defects of the unattained order lie hidden in a potential future while those of the actual world thrust themselves upon us. To remedy these defects is the goal of all socially-minded persons, but we do not come closer to this goal by a loaded presentation of the existing state of affairs. An unbalanced diagnosis is not a good preparation for therapy. We shall look at this diagnosis presently, but meanwhile let us note that the prescription rests on the prior assumption that the totally socialized society would also be a free one, a democratic one. If this assumption should not be sound, the whole case is lost.

Now, it is certainly not obvious that a fully socialized economy would or could be democratically conducted. Every impartial student of the history of government is aware that if you vastly increase the powers of the executive arm you increase the problem of making government responsive to the will of the people. A fully planned economy would run into that danger. It is the business of the thoroughgoing socialist who believes in democracy to show

how the danger can be met, not to deny that it exists. Yet the latter is the line that is almost invariably followed.

To ignore the danger altogether is to exhibit an unrealistic or biased attitude. Consider, for example, the case of a non-democratic country that adopts a system of total economic planning. Would the people of that country find it easier than before, or harder, to win democracy? Can anyone doubt that there would be grave new difficulties in the way? And if it is more difficult to attain democracy in a fully socialized economy, if also the actual rise of democracy owed much to the emergence of private economic power, is it not a reasonable position to admit that the problem exists, whether or not we think we have an answer to it?

Yet most advocates of thoroughgoing socialization not only ignore it but even speak prophetically of the great new freedom it will assure. To take one instance, Karl Mannheim called it "planning for freedom." Incidentally, he addressed this plea to semi-socialist England, which evidently is still in bondage. He promised it a number of new freedoms through over-all planning. Here, for example, is one. In an "unplanned society," freedom of choice in occupation is illusory. In a planned society, occupational choice would be determined by intelligence tests run by a board of experts. Then everybody would find his proper place and everybody would no doubt be happier, and of course more free.

It is so easy for all of us, scholars or statesmen, to credit the things that support our cause. Otherwise it would surely be difficult to maintain that people would feel more free if instead of choosing their occupations, within the limits of their opportunities and qualifications, the expert with a battery of tests did the deciding for them.

It is true that the occupational choice of the poor is more limited than that of the rich, but it is the way of every developing democracy to increase the range of opportunity. Complete equality of opportunity does not and cannot exist on this earth, but it is a distinction of democracy that it has enlarged it vastly more than has any other system and is still finding ways to enlarge it further. Democracy has always further work to do, and this particular work is eminently congenial to it.

The total planners make the assumption that a non-blue-printed society is a chaotic society. But societies achieve order through constant adaptation to changing conditions. This is the only kind of order that can be called free. Any intelligent society seeks to plan for each emerging situation, for each need as it arises or wins attention. There is always controversy over how any need should be met, but some kind of adjustment is made, better or worse according to the quality of the people and the character of the government.

These doubts, however, concerning the desirability of total planning are of less account than the great question-mark that throws its shadow over every program of this kind. The essential issue is not one of greater efficiency or less efficiency, not one of a more orderly or less orderly society, not one of the economic advantages or disadvantages of "free enterprise." However important these considerations may be, they are still not to be compared with the problem of the impact of power, the new power that full socialization inevitably puts into the hands of government.

2

The advocates of total over-all planning talk much of the power of big business and the power of high finance. They warn us of the dangers of concentrated private economic power; they would abolish it on that score. Certainly there is need for control to avoid such dangers, and an alert democracy will invoke various governmental controls for that purpose. But those who are alarmed by the perils of private power seem to have no fear of public power, no matter how vast and concentrated it may become. Thomas Hobbes said of Leviathan, the great state: "There is no power on earth that may be compared with it." The power of government is comprehensive and final, different in kind from any other power, more terrible in its abuse than any other power. It is armed with new techniques of control that make it potentially more formidable than it ever was in the past. Over many centuries men have learned to put a bit in the mouth of Leviathan. Will the bit hold it if political functions are vastly increased? Or will Leviathan enslave them again, as it does today in those countries which have abolished private economic power? When economic power and political power are totally combined, then there is no social *power* left in the community itself. Power has become monolithic. Can democracy restrain monolithic power?

If the total planners admit the problem at all they reply that there is always the people, the will of the people, to hold government in leash and make it their servant.

Is there not, however, a danger that something may happen to this will of the people? It is not a self-sufficing, self-maintaining thing. It needs appropriate conditions to manifest itself, to show vigor, to be stronger than the divisions out of which it always emerges. Can it exhibit that vigor when the executive arm of government becomes so overwhelmingly important? *Is there not a grave danger that when no power remains outside of government, government itself will rest on power?*

It is the unique quality of democracy that it puts consensus, expressed through the changing unstable majority opinion, over power, making power the agent of the greater will. The order under democracy is, first, consensus, from which authority is derived, in which power is then vested. Under all other forms of government the order is, first, power, from which authority is derived, to which in turn compulsive assent is given.

Democracy won its place, its high distinction, its uniqueness because those who believed in it and fought for it had acquired also some power of resistance against tyranny, some private economic power. The will of the people is the will of the groups that together constitute the people, groups of variant opinions and various interests, out of which majority opinion or public opinion emerges within the broader consensus of the democratic faith. If you take away the economic power of these groups and their organizations, including of course that of labor organizations, would the will of the people prevail against the new pressures of government? When all employment becomes in effect public employment? When producers have no longer any say about the volume or the prices of their products? When trade unions no longer have any say about their wages or the conditions of their work? For it is hard to see how they could still exercise these functions in a planned economy—or what would become of the planning?

These groups, it may be replied, will still be factors in decision-making, bringing their voices and their votes to bear on government, and the people as a whole can still by their votes determine the lines on which the government must operate.

But economic decisions are not easily determined by votes. Public opinion can determine only the broad direction of major policies. You can't run a business by plebiscites. Vital decisions are day-to-day affairs. They are executive decisions, and over matters of this kind appeals to the people are impracticable. Can the people decide how many automobiles are to be produced and how many pairs of shoes, and at what prices they shall sell?

There are deeper difficulties. They lie in the influences

and temptations of the new pervasive power. There is a malady of public spirit, of the will of the people, that is bred by this condition. High-minded men have spoken of the sickness of an acquisitive society, but at least there are many who find an escape from it. The sickness of a wholly planned society is one the effects of which none can evade. This sickness is likely to invade all the group organizations that otherwise might take a stand against the encroachments of power.

An organization consists of leaders and followers. The few must lead; the many can only follow, except that under favorable conditions they can choose their leaders.

Now, leaders are men with the power drive strongly developed. They could not come to the top unless they had the will to power and enough quality to make this will effective. They harness their power drive to the cause for which the organization stands. Thus leaders are animated by two more or less reconciled objectives: the success of the cause and their own success, their hold on power. Outstanding leaders have both attributes well combined and find a way of reconciling them satisfactorily. They are better leaders if they thoroughly believe in their cause but they are not likely to be leaders at all unless they thoroughly believe in themselves.

Now, with complete socialization the leaders of economic organizations and the directors of large-scale affairs are in a quite different situation from that of their counterparts in an open economy. It is now wholly to their interest to keep in well with the government. All positions of power have become governmental. Whether you head an industrial enterprise or a trade union—if trade unions as such continue to exist—you can no longer afford to break with the powers that be. You are in effect an agent of the government and you have no other place to go. In effect you draw your salary from the public treasury, and your status depends, as do your emoluments, on the favor of the government. Since only one power structure remains, you'd better stay inside.

A skeptical political scientist, Roberto Michels, laid down what he thought was a law of large-scale organization, the "iron law of oligarchy." He claimed that the leaders of left-wing or liberal organizations, once they get into power, gradually turn reactionary. Their ardor for liberty cools. Their devotion to the well-being of their fellow men slackens. The business of keeping themselves in power engrosses and changes them. They live and move in a new environment, the environment of an elite. They may have been sincere democrats to begin with, but the psychological effect of power and office is to turn them into oligarchs. They no longer belong to the people, but to the hierarchy. Michels supports his case by citing the example of various trade-union leaders, both European and American, and also of cabinet ministers who represented French and German left-wing parties. He concludes that the conditions and engrossments of leadership must always defeat democratic aspirations. "The orchestra is different but the music is the same."

Michels presents only one side of the case. It is a patent and gross exaggeration to say that democracy is always defeated by its leadership. But he does illustrate a tendency associated with the attainment of power. The possession of power, official power, bureaucratic power, tends to breed a corresponding outlook, so that the office ranks more than the service it renders and the official counts for more than the public he serves. This tendency is held in check in the more developed democracies. The politician learns to keep his ear to the ground. Public opinion does have weight and on the whole the people get the kind of legislation they want, a fact totally overlooked by Michels. Moreover, there is always an opposition ready and eager to expose and exploit the foibles, vanities, excesses, and aggressions of those in power. A vigilant democracy has ways of controlling its officials.

But would these controls still operate in a fully planned economy? The role of the executive would now be vastly increased and that of the legislature would in all probability be much diminished. Economic administration is inside work, expert work. The whole business of planning is administrative. It cannot be done by legislation. The public is inexpert, the legislator is inexpert—how could the public or the legislators they elect exercise effective control? The likelihood is extreme that the executive would dominate and make the legislature its mere agent. When the executive controls the whole intimately ramifying economic structure, it has tremendous opportunities to make itself supreme. And where the executive is supreme, there is an end of democracy.

The reply may be made that after all the executive itself, or at least its policy-making leaders, would still depend, given the democratic structure, on election by the people. But mere elections are no safeguard of democracy unless the conditions are present for the maintenance and development of an alert and critical public opinion. The danger is that the concentration of power in the executive would curb the emergence of any effective opposition, in which case elections would become as nugatory as those of Soviet Russia or of certain Latin-American republics.

The organizational impetus of this concentrated power would mean that the ambitious leader—every leader and every new aspirant to leadership—is now under strong persuasions to keep in step with the establishment. The roads to power and position and wealth all lead through government service. The multitude of boards and commissions and managerial positions ensure that leaders can climb the ladder only inside the establishment. Under these conditions Michels's iron law of oligarchy would come fully into its own.

Besides the leaders there are the rank and file; consider the new pressures that they in turn, bereft as they would be of independent leadership, must endure. You need new leaders to revolt from old leadership—would they have a chance to emerge? The usual democratic guarantees of civil rights would not suffice to protect workers who showed signs of independence. The constitution might proclaim that no one would suffer or be disadvantaged for his opinions; but it would now be very risky to rely on such a guarantee. There are so many grounds that could be alleged to justify demotion or punitive action. To whom could one appeal with much hope of success?

In short, when the government is the sole employer the word of the employer is law. There may be a façade of democratic liberties but there is inevitably a heavy disability attached to dissent, and conformity is the condition of every award. Moreover, there are more subtle influences that strongly abet the spirit of acceptance. Every means of communication is geared to the interests of government. Dissent becomes lonely and furtive and sinful.

It is a charge made against capitalist society that a few rich men control most of the newspapers and the other media of expression. There is some truth in the charge, though where democracy prevails every variety of opinion has its organs of communication and there is often scant relation between the number and circulation of the newspapers in favor of a particular party and the strength of that party at the polls. Anyhow, the remedy for the situation is not to be found by the "socialization" of the press. This solution involves the same innocent trust in the beneficent impartiality of an all-disposing government we have already commented on.

One planner, for example, writes that in the socialized

economy, in order to free the press and the radio from the control of monopolistic interests, he would put them in the hands of a body of public trustees. How curious, when in the planned society no monopolistic interests remain except the all-inclusive monopoly of government! The public trustees, he asserts, would ensure the freedom of these means of communication. How very curious, when under the conditions the only freedom urgently needed is freedom from subservience to the all-regulating, all-employing government! Who appoints the public trustees? Who pays them? We certainly hold no brief for newspaper magnates, but even they have to meet some competition, and anyhow they have to please the public. How when there is one magnate only, who has no competitor anywhere?

So, wherever we look around the socialized economy, we find only one recourse left against the not unreasonable fear that a government invested with such formidable powers may grow tyrannous, and that is the people's inherent devotion to an ideal, the ideal of liberty. But the people break up into men and groups who are under the strongest persuasions to be "loyal" to authority. The people are now disarmed. Their ground of resistance, their foci of independent economic organization, have been taken from them.

The reply may still be offered that even if all economic concerns are now determined by government the fundamental liberties, the liberties asserted in democratic constitutions, are not economic but cultural or spiritual liberties. So long as men have the liberty to think as they please, to worship as they please, to hold and express any views they please, to follow their own tastes, to join with their fellows, democracy is safe.

This defense does not come with very good grace from those who declare that "economic democracy" is more to be desired than "political democracy"—but let that be. It is enough to say that where government controls the career and the very livelihood of everyone the overwhelming premium on conformity applies not only to economic matters but to all others in which the government may be interested. Every government has a strong interest in the maintenance of the establishment. Every establishment is upheld not only by an economic doctrine but by a more inclusive creed that is favorable to its authority. There is therefore the gravest danger that even if democratic ideas prevailed at first, a creeping totalitarianism would spread over all the aspects of human life. Cultural and spiritual liberties do not dwell in the clouds, nor yet in the brave preamble of a constitution, but in the ways of life and habits of association to which the people are attuned.

3

The danger, then, is real—as real as the psychology of power. The advocates of total planning must tell us how the danger can be met, for it is frivolous to deny that it exists. And until they convince us that we can avoid the danger, should we not refrain from putting in jeopardy the democratic foundations of all our rights?

At best, only some urgent necessity would justify so gross a risk. What, then, is the necessity? For the sake of what great good must we imperil the hard-won legacy of ages, threatened as it also is by ominous world developments, the freedom of the spirit of man?

They speak darkly of dire dangers of another kind, dangers that only this total planning can avert. What precisely are they?

They speak of the "drift to fascism." What has elaborate planning to do with saving us from fascism? The well-established democracy has shown the power to resist and to overcome fascism. The threat is not immediate, and any more distant threat must be met by democratic vigilance, not by economic regimentation. The danger to liberty will not be met by reducing the area of liberty.

They speak of social disintegration. Whatever substance there may be in the charge, it is no easy ailment to cure and many and very diverse prescriptions have been offered. But it is reasonably sure that, so far as it prevails, this ailment is fomented by the detachment and helplessness of the individual in the face of the vast mechanized organization of modern society. Can you, then, restore the integrity of the individual by merging all voluntary and independent economic associations in one centralized organization of transcendent size? If on the other hand they attribute the ailment to the economic insecurity of the individual, I have already pointed out that the sufficient answer is the welfare state, which can exist perfectly well without the planned society.

They speak again of the increasing dominance of private interests, of financial and industrial empires, of ramifying cartels. Unquestionably there is need for vigilant control over these tendencies. But they make the assumption that democracy cannot control, cannot regulate them and therefore must take them over altogether. If democracy is not strong enough to regulate, how is it strong enough to run these industrial giants—and the incomparably greater giant of a wholly nationalized economy? Democracy has the obligation and the power to control the excesses of corporate enterprise. It has done much already in that direction. If it is enlightened to the need, it can do whatever needs to be done.

Under democracy part of the economy is always socialized and all the economy is subject to control. It controls whatever it has the will to control. If here and there it falls short, is that still not a lesser evil than to embark on a course which, once followed, is exceedingly difficult to reverse and which will assuredly imperil its very existence?

They answer: democratic control over big business is illusory. So long as private economic power remains it controls the organs of opinion, the press, the pictures, the radio, television. The big capitalists own the means of communication. What does liberty mean, what does public opinion mean, when all the weight of propaganda is on their side?

(And yet it is by propaganda—unless it should be by revolution—that they hope to win the people to their side!)

When one listens to such arguments, often enough coming from men of the highest principles, one wonders why we so often, all of us, can see only obvious half-truths or quarter-truths when the larger truth is equally obvious. Wealthy men and powerful syndicates do, for example, own the major newspapers—unfortunately it takes a lot of capital to run a big newspaper. But even the tiniest minority has its own means for spreading its opinions. Since the middle of the nineteenth century, in nearly all Western countries, there has been a persistent trend of opinion in favor of social legislation and generally in a "leftward" direction, and this trend has advanced with the majority of the greater newspapers on the other side. It is an interesting phenomenon of our own time that elections have again and again been won by the party or parties that had much less support from the press than the losing side received. In a democracy public opinion is alive and has its own momentum. It is never the mere tool of the big propagandists.

4

It is not the way of democracy to change by one stroke the whole order of things. Democracy does not work by blueprints. It pursues a course of continuous adaptation as conditions change and as its perception of needs changes. No hard and fast lines can be laid down to determine what government should take over, what it should curb, what it should regulate. But there are principles that can guide us, and in the first place there are broad distinctions to be made.

We should in the first place learn to distinguish more clearly between the welfare state and the socialist state. It is one thing that government should protect and insure and actively foster the health and security and general well-being of the people. It is an entirely different thing that government should take over and run the steel industry and the oil industry and the building industry and all the rest. When government can achieve its ends by proper regulation it may well be a confession of failure to nationalize instead.

There are of course special cases where it is desirable or necessary that government should take the responsibility for some area of economic activity. Such cases fall mainly into two types:

1. Where an industry is a natural monopoly of such a kind as to preclude effective competition while at the same time it is not amenable to effective price regulation if privately operated. This is a rather rare situation. It is more likely to occur in industrially undeveloped countries, when a new source of mineral wealth, say, is discovered. A present instance in the United States would be the manufacture and sale of the isotopes and other commercially utilizeable products of the atomic pile. Indeed, the present stage in the production of atomic energy in any form has characteristics that make it inevitably a state monopoly.

2. Where the economic returns from an industry, professional activity, or other service mature slowly over a long period, or where the full cost of such a service cannot properly be assessed against those who receive it, or where

the service itself has such wide implications for the national well-being that the latter would be impaired if the immediate beneficiaries were required to pay their proportion of the full cost. We have here a series of closely related conditions that everywhere have led governments to take responsibility for the supply of certain economic services instead of leaving them to private initiative. An obvious case is education, which is only modestly qualified by the fact that many governments permit private groups to provide it, in accordance with acceptable standards, alongside of the universal provision they make themselves. Other obvious cases are the post office and the highways, while various governments extend the area of public ownership to the railroads and other means of communication.

In this cursory sketch we cannot develop this theme. It is enough for our purpose to point out that if we apply the principles stated above with reasonable discretion, they leave intact a very considerable area of private economic power where the general regulatory function of government is sufficient to prevent any serious evils from private exploitation.

In short, the defects and weaknesses of our democracy on which the total planners enlarge do not call for the total planning they extol. Our democracy is not in such desperate condition that it needs to resort to this drastic surgery, which offers no assurance of the future health of the patient while it certainly threatens to kill him in the process of "recovery."

There is a kind of idealism that is three parts impatience and one part good intentions. It wants quick results and embraces whatever means may promise them. It falls in love with the means—they are so simple and clean-cut, so free from the ambiguities and perplexities of the social reality to which they are to be applied. Presently they confuse the goal with the means.

The goal is not socialism nor capitalism nor any neat blueprint of economic organization. The goal is the freer and fuller life of man in his society, equipped with all the means that liberate his capacities. Anything that advances this goal is to be welcomed. It is foolish to shout "socialism," "communism," when any particular measure is proposed which might further the end—when, for example, it is a question of some form of social insurance or protection against discrimination which would relieve men of anxiety or helplessness of any kind. It is equally foolish to approve any scheme because it means more planning or more socialism. Some people have a passion for planning. It is a passion for tidiness, a kind of social puritanism.

If instead we sincerely face each need as it arises the ever emergent society will not be capitalism, will not be socialism, but a flexible system far more suited for the promotion of human values and far more expressive of the particular genius of each people than any imposed and predetermined pattern. Democracy is the long emergent way, proceeding stage by stage, moving this way and that, sometimes hesitant and sometimes confused, but feeling the pulse of the ever changing present, always seeking, never fully attaining, never forgetting its own fallibility and never unwilling to correct its mistakes, always aspiring and never fulfilled. For such is the gift of life and such is the spirit that animates man.

V

The Meaning for America

1

I HAVE BROUGHT OUT the role played by private economic power in the evolution of democracy. I have shown that its role is not ended once democracy has come into being. I have pointed out how the transfer to the province of government of the entire planning and direction of the national economy would imperil the basic structure of our liberties and the creative thrust of free social energies. The investment of government with so much concentrated power, executive power, would become the gravest threat to our democracy. For the only material basis of resistance against the encroachments of government would be removed. Power is insatiate so long as it can find a way to expand, and unhappily, even in the best-established democracy, there are multitudes who are ready to take the side that promises the advantages and the emoluments of power.

But Americans may say: what has all this to do with us? In this country we believe in "free enterprise," we believe in limiting the sphere of government, we are committed to the maintenance of private economic power, so much committed that perhaps we are too ready to condone its abuses. And some may say this is not the lesson we need to learn. What we need is something more practical. We need guidance on how to keep private economic power, big business particularly, in its proper place.

No doubt we need more guidance on many things, including that. But it is of the first importance that we should

71

realize the true grounds on which we can effectively defend those things in which we believe. If we defend them on the wrong grounds, no matter how strong our belief, we defend them badly. The first thing we need to be more informed about is the nature of democracy. For now we are, in the eyes of the world, its leading defenders, and without our enlightened defense, democracy—and all the other things that belong with it, including private economic power—will suffer defeat perhaps over the whole earth.

In these times, when hostile dogmatists are swaying many peoples and grossly maligning us, when they are mocking the name of democracy by pinning it to their own despotisms, our lack of understanding is perilous. Recently during an election campaign the speaker most in demand all over the country by candidates belonging to one of the two major parties was a senator whose disregard of the principles of democratic fair play, as exemplified by the rash accusations he hurls at those who do not toe the same line as his own, is notorious. It is but one case out of many. Not only do our people have little conception of what democracy means but they are misled about it by too many of those who represent them.

We need in these crucial times to revise our list of deadly sins. We need to recognize how much more heinous than petty delinquencies is the misrepresentation of principles to gratify one's vanity or spite, or the betrayal of great causes by making them the cloak for personal advancement, or the debasement of high ideals by using them as a pretext for the calumniation of honorable men.

It is treachery to make a political football of the common cause or the common good. It is frivolous to be ignorant of what we profess to defend, and it is mischievous to defend it on mistaken or insecure grounds. The only thing that really binds men is a common trust, the only thing that unites them as a people is a cause they share. That cause must be something greater and deeper than mere interest. In these times it is not enough to hold aloft the banner of free enterprise. The cause for which men live, the flag for which they fight, must appeal to their hearts.

Let us take this lesson from our adversaries. They offer to the Western peoples not only security but also a faith, and to the Eastern they promise not only the land but also a vision. It is true they contradict their promise in all their policies, but they first win their way by proclaiming it. Lenin himself, the supreme technician of policy, knew he could not achieve his ends simply by playing up discontents, master as he was at that game. He knew he couldn't win the people over merely by stirring up hatreds or appealing to self-interest. They must feel the throb of a greater cause, they must glimpse a vision of a better world.

This vision is particularly necessary to win the loyalties of the young. We won't hold them, we certainly will not inspire them, if we make our case on the ground that capitalistic enterprise is more efficient than socialist planning. Efficient for what? The planners are sometimes efficient enough. The trouble with the communists is not their lack of efficiency. They may be too efficient, much too efficient, for our comfort. No, we must seek stronger and higher ground if we are to convince even ourselves, still more if we seek to persuade other peoples that ours is the better way.

That is why it is deplorable that in this country we are so superficial about our democracy. We do not appreciate the strength, the vitality, the depth and the breadth of the thing that makes us one. So our own faith in it is shallow and we carry little conviction when we are called upon by destiny to be the exemplar and the champion of democracy before the world.

Too often the "superior" people, the powerful people, the educated, the well-to-do, merely acquiesce in democracy, tolerate it, feel that it is necessary to save us from what might be worse. They are rather condescending about it. They are above the common level, and democracy gives voting power to the multitude, to the ignorant and to the poor. They are conscious of their superior ability and their superior wisdom. But they are not wise enough. They do not understand the problem of government. They do not understand that democracy is not a makeshift, a second-best, but the only solution of a many-sided problem. Democracy puts first the primary value, the potentiality in the human being for freer, fuller living. Democracy puts first the primary opportunity, the opportunity to realize this potentiality. Does this seem strange when, from whatever little eminence we have the luck to stand on, we look down at the stupidities and the superstitions that sway masses of men, at the passions of the crowd, at the inertia and indifference of the voter? That is the aspect which the superior are most likely to look on. But every other system than democracy, because it rests on power, must play on the ignorance and credulity of the people. Every other system, because it rests on power, must keep the people ignorant and in a condition of credulous subjection. Democracy alone brings the hope of liberation.

There are those again who take little stock in democracy because they are inveterately group-minded. The community as a whole seems to them to be nothing more than a bracket for the groups it encloses, and they often identify their social interest with one of these, with its success, with its dominance, with its struggle in relation to others. So they are mainly concerned with the welfare of the business group or the managerial group or a professional group or an artistic group and so forth, or more widely with the role or fate of the working classes or the middle classes.

There are of course interesting and important questions that focus in one particular group or another, but it shows lack of perspective to ignore on that account the welfare of the only integral social reality, the community itself.

The trouble about our American democracy is that so many of us take it so superficially and honor it so sentimentally. The sentimental side comes out in Fourth of July or Lincoln's Day orations. The superficial knowledge is apparent in the blurry tradition that turns democracy into the right to rise in the world, the right to make money and the right to be as good as one's neighbor.

For lack of the understanding of democracy our people do not see where the dangers to it lie. They are sometimes opposed to changes that would strengthen the hold of democracy and weaken the appeal of communism. Communism trades on our weaknesses, on our lack of understanding. It is unlikely that communism can make any more converts by appealing to its own merits—the facts are becoming too obvious. Therefore it redoubles its charges, its outrageous charges, against us; and if its propaganda has any success it is only because it exploits our weaknesses.

On the other hand, on account of these weaknesses we ourselves are unable to convince other peoples of the merits of our democratic way. We fail to convince them by our *example,* for reasons presently to be considered. Nor do we convince them by our *doctrine,* for we do not grasp it ourselves. We have had mighty little success in our appeal to the countries of the Orient, and reports from Germany suggest that we carry little conviction there. On the whole our pedagogues and missionaries for democracy have made a poor showing. The Voice of America has been slow in finding its pitch.

Away back in the war for independence, America won over thousands of captives to accept the justice of their cause. In the last World War the communists made some converts in their prison camps, under far worse conditions than those of our war prisons. But in our prison camps in this country, where many Nazi prisoners were held, we seem rather to have encouraged the diehards than to have converted the susceptible. The Nazis were all for order and discipline, and the people who ran these camps seemed to think that a kind of soulless order would suffice.

The United States cannot rise to its extraordinary opportunity and its extraordinary responsibility unless it understands better its own cause, unless it gives practical proof that it believes its own creed. Its weaknesses all stem from failure to be true to its creed. You cannot be true to what you do not understand, and many millions of modern Americans have never learned, have never been taught, to understand.

2

The weaknesses of our democracy are not weaknesses of democracy but of the lack of it. On the one hand we do not properly appreciate it, understand it. On the other, and in consequence, we do not sufficiently practice it.

So far we have been dealing with one aspect that is widely misunderstood: the relation of democracy to the economic system. It is a crucial aspect because those who hate and fear democracy ceaselessly exploit our lack of understanding here. Many of our citizens have not gone beyond the obsolete tradition of pre-industrial liberalism, a tradition that unfortunately many of our industrialists have taken over. They think democracy means individualism, rugged or otherwise, a free race and no favor, letting the devil take the hindmost. Whoever thinks that way understands neither the meaning of democracy nor the character of modern industrial society.

When we misunderstand such things we make mistakes in our policy that have grave practical consequences. We have been making such mistakes in our dealings with the peoples of the Orient. We invite them to join our side in the defense of democratic freedom. But the freedom we proclaim is for them an abstraction, without relation to their present conditions. Democracy has little meaning for those who live in total poverty. They must first find some way of release from that, before the gradual building of democracy can begin. They want liberation indeed, but first of another kind. They want liberation from an antiquated feudal subjection. They want their own earth. The communists promise them that. They want the vindication of their new sense of nationality, to be recognized and treated as equals. The communists promise them that. They believe the promises that are meaningful to them. The Soviets make such promises without scruple. We speak to them about the liberty of enterprise, confounding it with the liberties they need, confounding it with liberation from a grinding feudalism, and in the process revealing our own confusion about the meaning of democracy.

Capitalism and socialism are not the sheer alternatives they are often depicted. They are not total opposites in the sense in which democracy and totalitarianism are opposites. Let's keep the issues straight and not be bugabooed by words. Every modern society, as I have pointed out, is and must be socio-capitalistic, unless it goes over the verge and becomes communistic or adopts some other kind of wholly planned economy. The issue between capitalism and socialism is one of how far, how much of each, not whether or no. It is a question of intelligent discrimination. In every other domain of human activity, in every enterprise, in every art, it is necessary to learn to find an apt balance of various elements. It is so also in the political art, so far as partisan passions permit it to be an art. Here it is a question of where to draw the line so that liberty will still be safeguarded while human needs are still provided for.

But the issue between democracy and totalitarianism is quite different. Here there is no middle way, here no admixture is possible. Here are two irreconcilable opposites, suffering no compromise. Which does not mean that we must literally go to war with communism—in other words, with Russia and its allies. The conflict of systems would not be solved, but only brought into hideous confusion, by the war of peoples. There is no reason why we should not let them go their way if only they will allow us to go ours. But between the two philosophies or creeds or systems there is no give-and-take. Democracy perishes if it compromises with totalitarianism. You can no more mix the two than you can mix life and death, or liberty and terror. Whereas some socialism *must* be mixed with capitalism if capitalism is to survive. Indeed, pure capitalism is a dream, a deceiving myth. It nowhere exists—it never did, and never can, exist.

So we must avoid two gross fallacies: the fallacy of the left, the profound and soul-destroying fallacy that socialism means democracy, and the fallacy of the right, which has its own dangers and is a source of serious confusion, the fallacy that capitalism means democracy.

There is, however, another weakness of our democracy that is curiously entangled with the economic issue. Those who suffer because of it often associate it with capitalism, though there is no intrinsic relation between the two. At the same time it is a weakness that the communists make the most formidable count against us. There is little doubt that, in this country at least, communism has won its leading disciples among those who believe the communist propaganda that identifies capitalism with racial and ethnic discrimination and presents communism as alone free from group prejudice and class oppression. Here, indeed, they are able to exploit our gravest weakness, a weakness that more than any other undermines our influence and prestige throughout the world and our solidarity at home.

There is no such thing on this earth as a "classless society," and nothing on earth is remoter from the vision of it than is the Soviet Union. It began by massacring whole classes, the "bourgeoisie" and then the kulaks. Since then its ruling class has been uprooting, liquidating, or condemning to forced labor in the Siberian wilds group after group—Germans and Lithuanians and Latvians and Tatars and little free-spirited peoples of the Caucasus. The establishment of classlessness by terror is a hopeless enterprise.

The United States, or part of it, at one time came nearer to the vision of a classless society than any other country has come. It did not in fact abolish social class, but it took away its sting. It broke through the class-bound system that prevailed elsewhere. Something similar in degree happened in Canada, Australia, and New Zealand, but the process went farther in the American Middle West. There the detachment from Old World ties conspired with the availability of free hand to sever the connection between landownership and social class and thus to liberate the new communities from the rigidities and snobberies of class-bound Europe. The expanding frontier was not so individualistic or independent-minded in some respects as it has often been represented. Much of it was in the grip of a rather tyrannical sectarianism characterized by narrow morals and a nearly total lack of culture. But at least it was free from the spell of social class. As the Middle West grew in scale and importance its influence permeated widely, spreading the conviction that a man was no less worthy of respect because he was a merchant or a mechanic, that social class conferred no magic, that everyone had the right of opportunity, that a man was to be rated by what

79

he achieved, not by what he had been born to by way of inheritance or rank. This conviction was in turn eagerly embraced by the new immigrant groups, to whom America appeared as the home of liberty—liberty from class privileges and class restrictions.

The new American might envy, but he didn't kowtow. He might admire, but he didn't fawn. The common man had his own integrity, unsapped by the indoctrination of inferiority. He was not free from snobbery, but it was the snobbery of success, not of established class. If he looked up with envy, it was to something he might yet be himself. There was no predetermined worth, no inexorable status, of master or of servant, of owner or of worker.

This was a genuine liberation, for class consciousness limits a man's vision of humanity and takes away a part of his own humanity. In the higher-ups it breaks a facile complacency that has no relation to merit. In the lower-downs it breeds a furtive uneasiness that is falsely associated with demerit. Class consciousness drops a colored veil in front of all social reality, whether the reality be good or evil. It cannot look on persons as persons, it never sees the intrinsic qualities of people. Its standards of value are false and meretricious. It retards or distorts every generous advance of the human spirit, every co-operative enterprise. This conclusion holds whether it is class consciousness as preached by Karl Marx or class consciousness as practiced by the four hundred.

In America class consciousness shrank to small proportions. The sense of social class was superficial rather than fundamental. It was elastic, not rigid. It was personal, not corporate. No man felt he was born into a class. No man was educated to belong to a class. No man looked up to a class as his "betters," even if he still had the vanity to look down. This very considerable liberation from class consciousness was not only wholesome for the liberated;

it was also the source of a new kind of national vitality. It unloosed the creative force that comes from the free energies of a whole people, unbound by place or rank.

So complete a liberation had never been achieved before. England was the great exemplar of a broadening democracy, but though the power of class was broken, the prestige of class remained remarkably strong. There was a more fitful democracy set up in France, but there was relatively little social mobility, and family tradition and social station were limiting conditions. Some of the smaller countries, particularly the Scandinavian countries and some of the British commonwealths, moved in the same direction as did the United States. But the scale of the United States and the amplitude of its expansion and therefore of its social mobility gave its emancipation a greater momentum.

Thus was created the opportunity for a greater democracy than the world had ever known. How far it would be realized depended on the direction the newly liberated energies took and the degree of enlightenment that accompanied them. The United States moved along the road that was opened up for its people. But the advance was grossly retarded by a number of adverse forces. There was little training for democracy, the standards of education were low. With great new sources of wealth opening up, there was an undue emphasis on monetary success and a ruthless scramble to attain it. There was something worse than these things. The older-established groups, the dominant groups, the prestige groups found an ominous substitute for the ancient class hierarchy from which they had been delivered. There had remained one glaring contradiction to every proud claim of a new freedom: the existence of an inferior and partly segregated caste, the Negro. With this caste as its bottom tier a new stratification was built, based on "national origin" and on race.

On the one hand there was the shining ideology of a great openhearted democracy, in which all men might feel at home, all men of good will, whatever their ancestry. On the one hand there was the impulse to an "American way of life," a new and distinctive way, a rich and generous pattern of social living, too rich for any to comprehend, but generous enough for all to enjoy. On the other hand a dark shadow fell across this picture, the shadow of the oldest and worst servitude known to mankind.

Here, then, is the other weakness of American democracy —more than a weakness, for it is a rank betrayal of the democratic faith. By the time the newer immigration had spread throughout the land, rifts and cleavages had developed everywhere between more privileged and less privileged groups. The cleavage was deepest between the white and colored groups—the Negroes, the various Oriental groups, the Latin Americans, the American Indians—but there were rifts between the west European and the later immigrant groups, and a deep rift between the gentile and the Jew. Social prejudice and economic discrimination prevailed. Perhaps as many as forty million residents of the United States suffered some social or civil disparagement.

Only in the last decade or two have the people of the United States, outside of the groups thus affected, begun to waken to any realization of the problem. And although a number of states have passed anti-discrimination laws, and although the United States Supreme Court has come to view the Constitution as supporting the civil rights of the Negro, and although much is being written and spoken about the evils of discrimination, most of the people still fail to appreciate the intense hurt that our anti-democratic treatment of these groups is doing to our cause and to our country.

It hurts us in two very important ways. It lowers our

standing before the world, our influence in world affairs, our ability to win allies under the democratic banner. It defeats our claim to stand for democracy. It gives ammunition to those who wish us ill. Two thirds or more of the population of the earth are "colored," as we put it, and the members of these peoples are in this country treated as belonging to an inferior caste. How then can we hope to win to our side, no matter what our promises or our gifts, the peoples of the Orient, from the Philippines to Japan? How can we expect the great peoples of India and China to show favor to us or take our ideals seriously? How can we seriously promote a "good neighbor" policy with the peoples of Latin America when any of their members who cross the border to Texas or California are not allowed to eat in the restaurants or sleep in the hotels that are patronized by the superior race? True, we are beginning to reform. Some states in the Union rule out any such restrictions. But our record is bad, and we have still a great deal of "unneighborliness" and foolish pride of race to overcome.

Our discriminatory behavior hurts us also at home. To begin with, it entails a series of most unfavorable economic consequences, amounting to an enormous toll per annum. There are the costs of the denial of training and opportunity, of the loss of available talent, of the lower level of living and expectation, the poverty and the disease and the higher death-rate, among the groups that are most subject to discrimination, of the frustration and distortion of personality, of the needless duplication of facilities and services in the areas that practice segregation. It is no accident that in these areas the dominant groups themselves show the lowest indexes of per-capita income and of educational standards for the whole country. Beyond these costs there are the direct and indirect costs of the insecurity and disaffection caused by discrimination. It induces a state of mind in the discriminators that blinds them to the economic challenge to democracy. On the other hand it exposes the discriminated to the blandishments of communist propaganda. In our country and in our time discrimination against groups is more than an injustice, more than a denial of democracy; it is the grossest kind of stupidity.

We have begun to reform. Our people have in the last decade made a greater advance in this direction than in the previous fifty or sixty years. Many of them are beginning to glimpse something of the cost and the folly and the futility of it all. For the sake of our standing among the nations, for the sake of our unity as a people, for the safeguarding of our future against manifest perils, it is essential that we go much farther. We must abolish discrimination. Only so can we fulfill the meaning of America. Only so can our great tradition become anew a vital reality.

3

We live in a difficult world. One part of it, the part nearest to us in blood and in civilization, is impoverished by war, disoriented, distracted, insecure, cast down from its place of power. Another part of it, the largest part, is suffering from destitution and disease and overpopulation. It is also seething with unrest; its various peoples are rising to new consciousness of themselves and casting off old servitudes, whether to their own overlords or to the once imperial West. With its old needs and new desires the Orient stands at the turning of the ways, half responsive to the siren falsehoods of an unscrupulous power that conceals its own imperialism by attributing to us and to the West the most nefarious and inhuman designs. The remaining part of the world consists of this unfriendly power, a vast continent-embracing domain shut off from all contacts with us and continuously indoctrinated by a compulsive propaganda behind which terror lies in wait for heresy. It is ruled by a little group of fanatic or power-intoxicated men, who nevertheless fear us and fear their own peoples the while they clamantly assert that our cause is a lost one and our civilization is utterly decayed.

In such a situation our country might well be tempted to yield to the reflection of Hamlet:

> *The time is out of joint. O cursed spite,*
> *That ever I was born to set it right!*

Instead, it is called on, for the first time in its history, to sustain the whole civilization from which it sprang, and to thrust back the deadliest threat this civilization has ever faced. So tremendous an enterprise needs firmness and strength and patience and understanding—above all and prior to all else, understanding.

Concerning the most important things our people are grossly uneducated. When one sees how petty prejudice and partisan advantages distort great issues, when one listens to certain senators and representatives, when one hears their audiences applaud, when one thinks of the electorates that return them to office, when one reads certain newspapers that egg them on—one might wonder how we can ever rise to the call of history. We need understanding above all, and the strength that comes with understanding.

We need to take our democracy seriously—and proudly. For democracy, with its love for what we share in common, is itself no common thing, but a saving faith that is prouder than all other political faiths, making higher demands upon us. Democracy alone does not belittle humanity.

America's mission, if it can rise to the call, is to give a new translation of the ancient and ever new demand for the union of liberty and order, a new version of the philosophy of government incarnated in a way of life. The reason, the necessity, is so clear. America is both strong and free. Alone it combines these two precious gifts, strong in its resources, free from the terror that palsies thought and action over a third of the earth and from the poverty that debilitates most of the rest. On great and rare occasions it has fallen to some other people to save the world while saving itself. Now it is America's turn—if it also understands.

Index

Agricultural societies, economy of, 5–6

American democracy, weaknesses of, 72–8, 82–4

Authority: and wealth, 7–8, 9–11; effect of industrial change on, 16–18

Capitalism: industrial, 36; misrepresented by communism, 49–50; and socialism, not sheer alternatives, 77; confused with democracy, 78

City-state, 6, 7

Class conflict, in ancient Greece, 9

Classes, middle, role of, 12, 17–18, 21–4, 35–6

"Classless society": and Soviet Union, 79; vision of, in U. S., 79–80

Communism, 38–49

Community, sense of, lacking in Marxism, 45

Democracy: and private economic power, 15–17, 52–3; rise of, in England, 18, 20–6; and liberalism, 27; and Marxism, 39, 41–3; and socialism, 47–67; and economic planning, 55–67; lack of understanding of, 73–7, 85–6; and totalitarianism, 78

Discrimination, in U. S., 81–4

"Economic democracy," 53

Economic planning, 55–67

Economic power: in simple societies, 5; in agricultural societies, 6–7; in city-states, 6; in oligar-

Economic power (continued) chies, 8–11; reunited with political power, 43–4; as monopoly, 52

Engels, Friedrich, 37, 45

England: rise of democracy in, 20–5; and socialism, 48

Executive, role of, under economic planning, 62

Feudal society, 20

French Revolution, 28

Greece, ancient, 9, 18

Group-mindedness, 74–5

Hobbes, Thomas, 21, 58

Individualism, confused with democracy, 76

Industry, and social change, 11–14, 35–6

Insecurity, social, and communism, 42–3

Knights, Roman, 35

Labor, rise to power of, 14–15, 29

Laisser-faire, 26–7, 36

Landownership, ancient sanctity of, 15

Laski, Harold, 54

Latin-American republics, 9

Leadership, and economic planning, 60–3

Lenin, 38, 72

Liberalism, of eighteenth century, 26–7

Locke, John, 24

i

Mannheim, Karl, 54, 56
Marx, Karl, 9, 12, 32, 34, 37–47
Marxism, vs. communism, 43
Michels, R., 61
Monopoly, natural, 68

Oligarchies, relation of power to property in, 7–11
Oligarchy, iron law of, 61
Owen, Robert, 37

Power: in relation to property, 5–11; Marx's doctrine of, 41; communist system of, 45–6
Private economic power, 23–4, 52–3, 58
Property, and power, 5–11
Public opinion, and economic planning, 59, 62–4
Puritanism, and democracy, 22

Rome, 8, 9, 35
Rousseau, J. J., 28

Simple peoples, economy of, 4–5
Socialism: and welfare state, 29–30;

Socialism (*continued*)
earlier, 36–7; and democracy, 47–67; degrees of, 48–9; and economic power, 53–4
Socialization, and leadership, 6–61
Socio-capitalism, 77
Soviet Union: trades on weaknesses of democracy, 75; and "classless society," 79
Stalin, 45, 51
State, changing functions of, 29, 48–9, 58
Status: in relation to wealth, 11; and trade, 12–13

Technology: and social change, 12–14; and functions of government, 48–9
Totalitarianism, and democracy, 78
Trade, and social status, 12, 23

Victorian age, 32–3

Wealth, and authority, 8–9
Welfare state, distinguished from socialist state, 29–30, 68
Women, as communists, 39–40

A NOTE ON THE TYPE USED IN THIS BOOK

The text of this book has been set on the Linotype in a type-face called "Baskerville." The face is a facsimile reproduction of types cast from molds made for John Baskerville (1706–1775) from his designs. The punches for the revived Linotype Baskerville were cut under the supervision of the English printer George W. Jones.

John Baskerville's original face was one of the forerunners of the type-style known as "modern face" to printers: a "modern" of the period A.D. *1800.*

The book was composed, printed, and bound by The Plimpton Press, Norwood, Massachusetts.